BILINGUAL EDUCATION FOR LATINOS

Leonard A. Valverde, editor

Foreword by Donald R. Frost

Association for Supervision and Curriculum Development
1701 K Street, N.W., Suite 1100
Washington, D.C. 20006

Stock number: 611-78142
Library of Congress Catalog Card Number: 78-70710
ISBN 0-87120-092-9

Contents

ACKNOWLEDGMENTS

Publication of this booklet was the responsibility of Ron Brandt, Associate Director and Editor, ASCD publications. Nancy Olson provided editing and production services with the assistance of Elsa Angell, Patsy Connors, Anne Dees, and Constance Clárk.

Special thanks are extended to the Museum of Modern Art of Latin America, Organization of American States, Washington, D.C., for permission to use in this booklet works of art from their permanent collection and from special exhibits.

Foreword

The authors have performed an outstanding service for educators through the creation of an excellent primer for program developers of bilingual education for Latinos. The monograph provides valid guidelines and models to be followed in meeting the challenge of educating the second largest and fastest growing minority population in the United States. Fulfilling their purpose as stated in the Preface, they provide a comprehensive theoretical understanding of bilingual education and present practical information about program implementation.

Chapter 1 is rich in statistical information which is helpful in understanding the topic. It proposes philosophical guidelines with rationale for program development. This chapter is highly recommended for all educators whether or not they are involved in bilingual programs.

Chapter 2 reinforces the premise that many of the valid criteria for curriculum development for monolingual programs are also applicable to bilingual programs. However, certain criteria are identified as crucial when applied to bilingual programs and are fully explained with suggestions to be followed.

Chapters 3, 4, and 5 discuss the identification of students, the selection and training of staff, and the supervision of instruction and programs. Descriptions of appropriate existing tests to assess language competence along with potential problem areas in the use of test results are presented. Valid suggestions for staff selection and training as well as a strong emphasis on the need for program supervision are also included.

Chapter 6 strongly emphasizes the need to work with the community and suggests ways in which this can be done. The information presented here will lead to a greater understanding of the Latino culture.

Chapter 7 summarizes bilingual education, and reminds us that we must not lose sight of the major goal of public education: to accept students where they are and to acknowledge individual differences.

The monograph will be useful to all educators involved in bilingual educational programs. It is rich in ideas and guidelines which will help educators gain a greater understanding of Latino educational concerns. There is something here for everybody.

DONALD R. FROST, President, 1978-79
Association for Supervision
and Curriculum Development

Preface

Chicanos, Puerto Ricans, Cubans, Mexicans, and Central and South Americans, all Latinos yet all Americans, all alike yet all different, all retaining their culture yet all changing. The Latino population of the United States is on the verge of becoming an influential, if not a decisive force in shaping the character of American education. Three reasons, embedded in the lead sentence, give credence to the proposition of potential power.

First, the American citizenry of Hispanic ancestry, especially the school-age population, is increasing faster than any other ethnic minority group in the United States. Concurrently and with little notice, the Latino population has passed from a regional to a national group. The common misperception of Mexican Americans isolated to the Southwest, Puerto Ricans segregated to the Northeast, and Cubans restricted to Dade County, Florida, is slowly but surely dying. In every major urban school district, educators are finding sizable numbers of Hispanic students, and the percentage is steadily growing in suburban and rural school districts as well. Second, more and more the prevailing practice of America's ethnic and racial groups is to take pride in holding onto their culture. The Latino is very much anchored to this philosophy of cultural maintenance. Third, just as there are characteristics common to the various Latino groups (the most obvious being the Spanish language), there are other characteristics which reveal their rich diversity. The pluralism stems from such factors as culture, manifested in customs and nationality, reflected by history. Not only is there intergroup diversity but there is intragroup diversity as well; Latinos represent heterogeneity at its best and finest.

What are the implications? What influence will these three facts have on education? What effect will these factors have on the education in the United States in the near future? Because of the increased number of Latino students, school people will be unable to ignore the need for altering instructional programs to better serve Latinos and other culturally different young people. One certain reality will be the expansion of bilingual education not only to include more Latinos but other students, the nonEnglish as well as the English-speaking student. Furthermore, the educational philosophy of American education will have to change from the already eroding ethnocentric viewpoint to a pluralistic perspective, in order to accommodate the true multicultural fabric of today's and tomorrow's society. Simultaneously, the national educational policy will have to be pluralistic, founded on the dimension of culture. Educators will no longer be able to view Latinos as a homogeneous group but as individuals.

With these assumptions seen as near realities, *Bilingual Education for Latinos* was conceived and nurtured. More specifically, it was written to provide a comprehensive theoretical understanding about bilingual education and to present practical information about program implementation. As editor and as one particularly concerned with improving the education of Latino children, I am gratified with the contribution this book makes, but at the same time painfully aware of the inadequacy of this lone effort when compared to the challenge facing all educators. Therefore, it is the sincere hope of the contributing authors and the ASCD Latino Working Group on Bilingual Education that this monograph will motivate ASCDers and others to move decisively and assertively forward to better the educational condition of all ignored children.

As chairman of the Latino Working Group, I wish to acknowledge a few individuals for their support. Gratitude is owed to Gordon Cawelti and the Executive Council for responding to the defined needs and interests of Latinos both in ASCD specifically and in education generally. Special thanks are extended to David Ballesteros and Rosa Castro Feinberg for their moral support.

LEONARD A. VALVERDE

1.
Bilingual Education and the Latino Student
Meliton Lopez

In recent years, the Latino student has been the subject of dramatic, and at times traumatic, educational challenge in the nation's schools. A large number of Latino students now seek a viable educational opportunity in schools which have traditionally operated on a monolingual-monocultural basis. The diversity of this Latino population in terms of national origin and language demands changes heretofore foreign to American schools. Predominant among these changes is the emergence of bilingual-bicultural education. Though still in a pioneering stage, bilingual-bicultural education can be a meaningful alternative in meeting the needs of the diverse Latino student population.

The United States Latino population is no longer confined to a few geographic locations. Nor is the Spanish-speaking/Spanish-surnamed student population confined to any one national origin. They do not comprise an easily identifiable ethnic/cultural group. The number of Latinos living in the United States is officially figured at 11 million [1]; however, current estimates by some authorities indicate that there are 20 million Spanish-surnamed people in this country.[2]

Of the official 11 million accounted for in the 1976 U.S. Census, 6.6 million are Mexican American, 1.8 million are Puerto Rican, and 2.4 million are Cuban, Central American, and South American.[3] The same

---

[1] U.S. Bureau of the Census. "Current Population: Persons of Spanish Origin in the U.S., March 1976." Series P-20, No. 302. Washington, D.C.: U.S. Government Printing Office, 1976.

[2] Carmela Locayo. "Hispanic Educational Development." Speech before the Association of Mexican American Educators Convention, Long Beach, California, November 12, 1977.

[3] U.S. Bureau of the Census, *op. cit.*

census report indicates that virtually every Latin American country from Mexico to Argentina is represented as the place of origin for the U.S. Latino student population.

Latinos are no longer confined to a few metropolitan urban centers of the Southwest. The 1970 census indicates that Latinos are found in every state, including Hawaii and Alaska. The three major Latino groups found throughout the United States are Mexican Americans (Chicanos), Cubans, and Puerto Ricans. Mexican Americans are found predominantly in the Southwest and Midwest (Great Lakes region), but also in every large city. Mexican Americans also comprise the greatest number of migrant farm workers throughout the agricultural regions in the nation. Cubans are found in greatest number in Miami Beach and other large cities in Florida. However, many Cubans also reside in Los Angeles, New York, Chicago, and other urban centers. The Puerto Rican population is primarily confined to the large metropolitan centers of the Northeast— New York, Boston, Trenton, and Atlantic City, but again Puerto Ricans are found in almost every major city in the country. Latinos from every Latin American country can be found in practically every state and every city in the United States. Their occupations range from medical doctors and lawyers to migrant workers and domestics. Collectively, this population comprises the second largest minority in the country.

Because of the diversity of national origins, it is difficult to ascertain the exact number of Latinos from each of the Latin American countries. We do know that on a continuum we have Latinos (mostly of Mexican ancestry) who are second only to native Americans as our earliest residents and some who are relative newcomers. Additionally, because of the proximity to Mexico and the ease with which Latinos can enter the United States there is a constant flow of immigrants.

Latinos have been able to maintain a variety of linkages with their mother countries while at the same time adapting to a new environment. Some Latinos have practically renounced their cultural and linguistic heritage while others cling tenaciously to their cultural accruements and language. Thus, Latinos are complex, as individuals and as a group.

As the fastest growing minority in the United States, Latinos are also a very young population. The median age of Latinos is estimated at 20.9 as compared to 28.9 for the nation as a whole. Thirteen percent of the Latino population is under the age of five. By the latest count, Latinos account for one out of every 20 persons in the United States. Demographic predictions indicate that their accelerated birthrate will, by 1981, make them the majority in California and in most of the Southwest. Carlos Ovando writing in the *Phi Delta Kappan* in December 1977, stated that this demographic pattern is being felt throughout the 10 states which have a large concentration of Latinos. For example, in the Los Angeles schools during the nine year period from 1966 to 1975 there was a 50% increase in the Latino student population. New York, Florida, Illinois, and New Jersey are experiencing similar increases. Expansion in the midwestern states has been estimated at 110% between 1960 and 1970.[4]

Despite its diversity and vitality, the Latino population, in general, is not doing well in American schools. Except for native Americans, they have the highest dropout rate among the minorities in the United States. Their educational attainment is below that of whites, blacks, Asians, and all other minorities except native Americans. The National Assessment of Educational Progress, in its May 1977 report, examines the achievement of Latinos ages 9, 13, and 17 in the areas of social sciences, science, mathematics, career and occupational development, and reading. The report concedes that Latino achievement is consistently below the achievement of the total national population and of white students.[5]

Many authorities appear to agree that the traditional monolingual/monocultural approach of American schools is much the cause of the Latino population's educational plight.[6] Past educational practices maintained a posture of "Americanizing" the children of the nonEnglish-speaking residents and immigrants. This practice continues into the present, though often less harsh in tone. Children who are linguistically and culturally different have been expected to acquire a new language system and master the scope and sequence of the typical school curriculum at the same pace and rate as the native speakers of English. This unrealistic expectation has led to frustration, confusion, and trauma for many Latino students and parents. Often students are left to "sink or swim" in the torrent of an alien school environment.

At other times, an effort has been made to provide English as a Second Language (ESL) instruction. However, the ESL approach is limited because it does not take into account cognitive and affective development. The students are involved in the acquisition of English as a language, but are falling academically behind. This causes an academic retardation or an academic void which may never be filled even after the child has acquired sufficient command of English to function in the regular cur-

---

[4] Carlos Ovando. "School Implications of the Peaceful Latino Invasion." *Phi Delta Kappan* 59(4):231; December 1977.

[5] National Assessment of Educational Progress. *Hispanic Student Achievement in Five Learning Areas: 1971-1975.* Dept. #BR-2. Washington, D.C.: U.S. Government Printing Office, May 1977.

[6] Thomas P. Carter. *Mexican Americans in School: A History of Educational Neglect.* New York: College Entrance Examination Board, 1970. pp. 16-27.

riculum. Because of this set-back, parents and leaders of the Latino community began and continue to press for bilingual education as a means of obtaining a better educational opportunity for their children.

In 1974, the movement for bilingual education produced a landmark decision by the U.S. Supreme Court in the *Lau* v. *Nichols* case. The Court unanimously agreed that there "is not equality of treatment merely by providing students with the same facilities, textbooks, teachers, and curriculum; for students who do not understand English are effectively foreclosed from any meaningful education." [7] Thus, the Court reiterated that "there is nothing less equal than the equal treatment of unequals." [8]

The Court's decision made it imperative that the schools of the nation provide a program that would not prevent nonEnglish-speaking students from receiving a meaningful education. The Court demanded that districts "fashion appropriate relief" to rectify the language deficiency in order to open instruction to students deficient in English language skills.

While the Supreme Court did not specify or dictate that bilingual/bicultural education be the vehicle by which a meaningful education be provided to the nonEnglish-speaking students, subsequent lower court cases have indicated it should be.

The Supreme Court's decision was handed over to the U.S. Office for Civil Rights which developed a document, the so-called Lau Remedies.[9] It was dictated by the Lau Remedies that bilingual education be a vehicle to correct past practices (found unconstitutional by the Court) in the education of the nonEnglish-speaking student.

Subsequent lower court cases also indicated that bilingual education was viewed as a viable means of fulfilling the law of the land regarding the education of nonEnglish and limited English-speakers. Three Court cases are important: (a) *Serna* v. *Portales Municipal Schools,* (b) *Aspira of New York, Inc.* v. *Board of Education, City of New York,* and (c) *Keyes* v. *School District No. 1, Denver, Colorado.*[10]

In the *Serna* case, the Circuit Court ruled that bilingual instruction is a remedy to meet the Lau decision. The Court stated that, "a student who does not understand English and is not provided with bilingual instruction is therefore precluded from any meaningful education." This

[7] *Lau* v. *Nichols,* 414 U.S. 563 (1974).

[8] *Ibid.,* p. 3.

[9] Office for Civil Rights. *Task Force Findings Specifying Remedies Available for Eliminating Past Educational Practices Ruled Unlawful Under Lau v. Nichols.* Washington, D.C.: Department of Health, Education, and Welfare, Summer 1975.

[10] Joseph Grant. "Bilingual Education and the Law: An Overview." Austin, Texas: Dissemination and Assessment Center for Bilingual Education, no date.

was the first time that a court expressly required bilingual education as a remedy.[11]

In the *Aspira* case, consideration was given to who should receive bilingual instruction. The Court ruled that all Hispanic students should be given a test to determine their proficiency in manipulating the English language. Those students scoring above the 20th percentile were presumed competent in English and in no need of bilingual instruction. Those scoring below the 20th percentile were to receive bilingual instruction provided their Spanish proficiency exceeded their English language facility.[12]

The *Keyes* case, in Denver, was a desegregation case. However, this is an important case because of the fact that a bilingual education program was part of the desegregation plan. The Court praised and approved the bilingual program as a desegregation option where students who were nonEnglish-speakers must receive instruction in academic areas in their native language (in this case, Spanish) until they could compete effectively in English.[13]

By lower court interpretation, then, bilingual education appears to be a viable educational alternative to ensure Latino students success in school. It is important at the onset to recognize that bilingual/bicultural education is a viable educational endeavor for every student, Latino or nonLatino, Spanish-speaker or nonSpanish-speaker.

It is important to keep in mind that bilingual/bicultural education is defined as: "a program of instruction which uses two languages for instruction, one of which is English. The program also pays particular attention to the heritage and cultural background of the students it serves." [14] Since English is one of the languages which by definition must be used in a bilingual/bicultural program, it is imperative for practitioners to understand the extent to which and also when English and the other language should be used. In order to determine this, the student's language dominance must be assessed. There are a variety of ways this can be accomplished. For the elementary age child in the primary grades, a variety of easy to administer instruments is available.[15] At the secondary level the

[11] *Ibid.,* p. 11.

[12] *Ibid.,* p. 24.

[13] *Ibid.,* p. 24.

[14] Title VII Bilingual Education Programs, United States Congress, Public Law 93-380, 1968.

[15] Among the tests which can be used are: the *Bilingual Syntax Measure,* (BSM), Houghton Mifflin Company; *Bilingual Inventory of Natural Language,* (BINL), check parts system, San Bernardino, California; *Gloria and David Test,* San Diego State University, San Diego, California; and *San Diego Observation Assessment Instrument,* San Diego City Schools, California.

task is more complicated because the instruments are limited in number and reliability.[16]

However, this should not excuse the educator from trying to do his or her best to ascertain the most beneficial instructional language to use. Once the instructional language of the students is ascertained, the curriculum can be implemented with a greater degree of certainty for success.

Often Latino students find themselves in an alien school environment where the familiar sounds of their language and the predictability of behavior based on their cultural backgrounds are non-existent. Frank Voci sees these students as being in an altered state of consciousness.[17] This "altered state" is characterized by high anxiety, apathy, fear, and mistrust.

The limited and nonEnglish-speaking Latino students enter schools with a variety of educational backgrounds. They often come from fine schools in Mexico and Latin America and are quite advanced in their studies. Others enter schools with limited educational experiences and still others have no experience with any kind of schooling at all. For all of these students, their lack of familiarity with and their inability to manipulate the English language present a handicap. The school is a verbal world and it is by means of that verbal communication that a major portion of any child's education takes place. Failure to understand and function in that verbal world limits the amount of knowledge, information, and skills a child can gain.

As stated earlier, it is not uncommon for most teachers to expect nonEnglish and limited English-speaking children to master the curriculum at the same rate and sequence as native English-speaking children and at the same time to acquire a new language in the process.[18] This expectation is clearly unrealistic as evidenced by the high dropout rate and the low educational attainment of the Latino population.[19] Culture also plays an important role in the Latino child's educational experience. The value system which children bring to school and the cognitive style which their culture has imbued in them often are at variance with that of the school.[20]

[16] Editor's note: See Chapter 3 for discussion of the language assessment of the nonEnglish-speaking student.

[17] Frank Voci. "Biculturalism: An Altered State of Consciousness." Presentation to Association of Mexican American Educators Convention, Long Beach, California, November 13, 1977.

[18] Carter, op. cit., p. 49.

[19] U.S. Commission on Civil Rights. "The Unfinished Education." Report 2. Washington, D.C.: U.S. Government Printing Office, 1971. pp. 8-9.

[20] Manuel Ramirez, III, Alfredo Castaneda, and H. P. Leslie. Mexican-American Values and Culturally Democratic Educational Environments, Systems and Evaluations in Education, Riverside, California, 1972. Austin, Texas: Dissemination Center for Bilingual Education, 1973.

Because of this variance, often unconscious, cultural clashes occur between teachers and Latino students.[21]

Traditional educational philosophy (mono-culture and English-only instruction) is ineffective and accounts for the aforementioned high dropout rate among this student population. Historically, the school saw its role as one of socializing the children who were culturally and linguistically different. Thus the "Americanization" process took place by a philosophic stance that was basically exclusionary in nature. It excluded the language and culture of the child in the belief that the "melting pot" approach was sound and defensible.

An outgrowth of this philosophy has been the practice of leaving Latino children to succeed or fail on their own in the verbal world of the school. Other common practices have been the pullout ESL approach in the elementary schools and an ESL period or two at the secondary school level. These practices have proved ineffective primarily because ESL teachers are often not trained in the philosophy and techniques of second language acquisition.

While learning English via limited ESL instruction, the Latino child is receiving little or no academic/intellectual stimulation. As a result, the child falls farther and farther behind in academic and affective development. And, the child's sense of worth and sense of efficacy are often diminished.

What is needed is an educational approach that takes into account the Latino child's need to develop cognitively and affectively while in the process of mastering the English language. Such an educational approach can be bilingual/bicultural education. This approach calls for a conceptual framework that takes into account the following assumptions:

1. The learning of one's mother tongue takes place in the intimacy of one's family and carries with it memories, feelings, and emotions which become part of the self.

2. The acceptance and valuing of the pupil's native tongue nurture feelings of acceptance and valuing of self and family.

3. Human beings learn to listen and to speak before they learn to read and to write. Thus, the natural order of language learning is listening, speaking, reading, and writing.

4. It is imperative that the student read first in the language which has been orally mastered at home.

[21] Leonard Olguin. *Unconscious Cultural Clashes.* San Jose, California: Santa Clara County Department of Education, 1968.

5. There is an important relationship between oral language and its written form, for writing depends on the prior existence of speech.

6. Learning to read and to write in Spanish makes full use of the mastery of sound and structure of the native language which Spanish-speakers possess. The introduction of the written form of a second language, English, unrealistically demands responses to sounds and structures not sufficiently controlled in the oral form.

7. Use and refinement of one's native language opens up the content areas of math, science, literature, and all other facets of the curriculum which demand the processing of information presented through print.

8. A broad base of oral language should support any writing system to be learned if both oral and written language proficiency are the goals.

9. There are many possibilities for positive transfer to the reading of English after literacy is achieved in Spanish. These transfer elements stem from the commonalities in the reading process as well as the attitudes of learners who have been successful and who know they are literate.

10. In today's world, there is a tremendous need to encourage literacy and language proficiency in many idioms. Many future linguists of our nation may be found among the present Latino student population.[22]

In addition, the conceptual framework of bilingual/bicultural education should address itself to accomplishing the following goals:

Cognitive Domain

1. To provide expanded encounters with the environment so that concepts may be acquired and clarified

2. To extend the refined oral production of the native speech of the pupils

3. To develop literacy in the native language of the learner

4. To present the sounds and structures of English for second language acquisition in its spoken form

5. To offer literacy in the second language commensurate with mastery of oral English

6. To support achievement in the content areas of math, science, social studies, etc., through the use of the learner's native language to mediate meaning.

Affective Domain

7. To enhance the pupil's self-esteem through the provision of successful experiences

[22] Eleanor Thonis. *Marysville Bilingual Education Project Evaluation.* Marysville, California: Marysville Reading Center, 1968.

8. To nurture a sense of pride in the pupil's language, heritage, and culture through the inclusion of the Spanish language and the respective culture of the group in the curriculum

9. To prevent discouragement, failure, and withdrawal among pupils who have often felt alienated in the traditional school curriculum

10. To ensure achievement in the subject areas sufficient to prevent educational retardation while pupils are gaining control of the oral and written forms of the language of the curriculum offered in English

11. To create opportunities for developing truly literate and functionally balanced bilingual citizens.

Language is learned in the intimacy of one's family and around those we care about and cherish. It is in these comfortable surroundings that we express our most intimate feelings and emotions. Educators must accept and nurture, both verbally and nonverbally, the language children bring with them from the home. In doing this, not only do we indicate that the child's language is worthwhile, but also that the child is a worthy individual. As children sense this worth, educators can help them develop and reinforce a sense of efficacy.

The native language a child brings to his or her first school experience is a precious possession, and it is equal to the English language. The native language is a viable means of communicating, receiving input, processing and storing and retrieving concepts, information, and knowledge. No child is alingual. Children come to school with a language system that helps them cope with their environment. The school must use the child's native language as the mediator between the child's culture and that of the school and larger society.

The child's native language is the initial means by which literacy skills are taught to the child. It is also the foundation for cognitive and affective development. While the native language is initially essential for academic development, English as a Second Language (ESL) should be used to develop English language skills.

Writing is an abstract form of talking, and reading is an abstract form of listening. A child cannot read that which he or she cannot hear. Therefore, in the instruction of ESL, the school must provide a variety of language development opportunities in order to instill in the child new phonology, morphology, and syntax in addition to vocabulary.

The possession of a language other than English is not a deterrent to learning English or acquiring, forming, and developing concepts. But it must be remembered that the child's native language can present phonological interference factors for the child in hearing and producing the sounds of a second language.

Children who are linguistically and culturally different are not deficient persons. They bring with them a rich background in terms of culture and language. Our expectations for the culturally different child must be no different than for children of the dominant language.

Furthermore, without accepting the following assumptions, based on research and common sense, bilingual education becomes useless:

1. A child cannot be expected to read and understand material in a language that he or she has not mastered in the oral form.

2. A child whose language is other than English cannot be expected to master the language and the scope and sequence of the school curriculum at the same time and at the same rate as native speakers of English.

3. An English as a Second Language (ESL) or Teaching English to Speakers of Other Languages (TESOL) only approach is not sufficient for the nonspeakers or limited speakers of English. These approaches provide for the acquisition of English as a language. However, while the child is learning English as a language he/she is falling behind academically, resulting in academic retardation.

4. A child cannot acquire, form, or develop concepts through the medium of a language which he or she has not mastered in the oral form.

5. A child only learns to read once. A child transfers academic and literacy skills learned via his or her native language to the second language once the second language has been sufficiently mastered.

Philosophically the conceptual framework takes into account three inseparable, interlocking areas of the child's background: culture, language, and cognition/affection.[23] (See Figure 1.)

In the area of *culture* the following elements are to be considered and interwoven into the curriculum:

Values—the outward, overt manifestations of universal values such as respect, affection, rectitude, well being, responsibility, skill and understanding

Traditions—holidays, celebrations, customs

Arts and crafts—the aesthetic expressions of a people in traditional modes

[23] Rosa Kestelman, Susan Maiztegui, and Meliton Lopez. *Conceptual Framework for Bilingual/Bicultural Education.* Teacher Corps, Cycle VII. Santa Cruz: University of California, 1971.

Figure 1.
Bilingual/Bicultural Framework

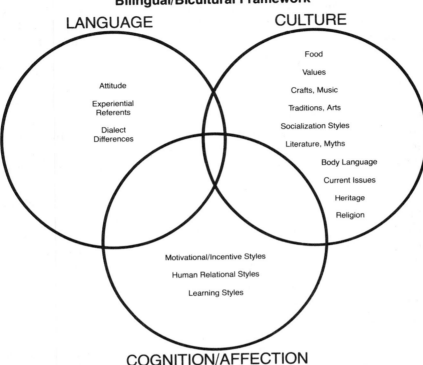

Music/dance—folk music and dances which are part of the artistic traditions of a people

Socialization styles—the mode in which the culture teaches its members

Food—the traditional cuisine, staple as well as luxurious foods

Religion—the role the church plays in the daily life of the people

Myths—folklore, beliefs, tales, and stories

Heritage—contributions made by Latinos to the totality of American culture and the world community, as well as accomplishments of the group's forebears

Literature—imaginative stories real and fictional that give substance to the reading program

Body language—the nuances and meaning that Latinos give to their body movements as a means of communication

Current issues—education, unemployment, discrimination, labor, the farmworkers' struggle, and various movements including women's liberation.

In the area of *language,* three elements are to be considered:

1. Dialectical Differences—Latinos come to school speaking a wide variety of dialects of Spanish. All of these dialects are similar to so-called standard Spanish. Anyone who really speaks Spanish will be able to understand and communicate effectively with a Latino who has a different dialect. The important point is to have a positive attitude toward the child's language. If one considers the function of language, then it is easy to deal with this point. Language is to communicate, and it becomes part of the self. To accept an individual's language is to accept him or her. Conversely to reject an individual's language is to reject him or her. The framework considers the language which the child brings to school the foundation upon which to build a solid language base via a native language arts program and a carefully planned second language acquisition program.

2. Experiential Referents—Latinos, as other students, come to school with a wide range of experiences in their language development. Some come from rural backgrounds, others come from urban areas. Each has had different encounters with his or her environment, and therefore there are differences in vocabulary, structure, syntax, and experiences.

3. Attitude—First is the attitude of the parents toward the function of the school. Many Latino parents feel that the children should not be taught in Spanish at school. They are firmly convinced that the child should be exposed only to English during the course of the school day, mistakenly believing that the child will progress faster if he or she is exposed to an English only curriculum. Thus, it becomes a function of the school to educate the parents to the benefits of bilingual education. A second consideration in dealing with language is the attitude of the child. Often educators find that children will not speak Spanish even if that is the only language they know. They fear being different and will remain silent rather than use their Spanish. Other students, especially at the secondary level, find that English is a difficult language to master and will develop a very negative attitude often leading to a refusal to learn and use English. It becomes the bilingual teacher's task to deal realistically with attitudes held by Latino students and help them and their parents to evaluate their attitudes and actions.

The area of *cognition/affection* takes into consideration research dealing with cognitive styles. Research findings indicate that because of the respective culture which nurtured respective groups, individuals tend to have: (a) a preferred way of learning, (b) a preferred way of teaching, (c) a preferred way of communicating, and (d) a preferred way of relating to one another.[24] These four attitudes form our preferred motivations, incentives, and interpersonal relationships. It is important that these aspects of a child's personal accruements be taken into account in the design of a bilingual/bicultural curriculum.

Once the basic framework is accepted, the logical next step is to design the delivery system which will best serve the needs of the limited and nonEnglish-speaker. If academic excellence and English language acquisition are primary goals for the Latino child, attention should be given to the language capabilities of Latino students. Conversely, if academic excellence and Spanish language acquisition are the goals for the native English-speakers in a bilingual/bicultural program, the same language consideration should be exercised for them.

Invariably, an analysis of the results of the language dominance testing will reveal that there are four major instructional groups in the bilingual/bicultural program. These are: Monolingual Spanish-speaker, Monolingual English-speaker, Predominant Spanish-speaker, Predominant English-speaker.[25] For instructional purposes it is recommended that the programs for these four groups be as indicated in Table 1.

Once the student acquires bilingual skills and can function on a somewhat equal level in both languages, some philosophical, political, and economic decisions have to be made. The students (Latinos and nonLatinos) now have at their disposal a great asset, the facility to function in and manipulate two languages. Further, they have the ability to understand and function in two cultures with a high degree of success. They have internalized some important cultural dimensions from both the mainstream culture of the United States and the Hispanic culture. A question must then be asked: Should these skills be abandoned in favor of an all English language curriculum? While the decision should be based on a philosophical premise, more often than not the decision is made based on political and economic factors.

The philosophical considerations should be based on the inherent value of language itself. If language is viewed as a resource of intrinsic value which enhances an individual's personhood and which becomes an asset to the nation, then a decision will be made to maintain the two languages. Thus students proceed in their educational endeavors maintaining and refining their two languages until graduation from high school.

The maintenance of two languages can be achieved in a wide variety of organizational patterns:

[24] Manuel Ramirez, III, Alfredo Castaneda, and Herald P. Leslie. *Introduction to Cognitive Styles, Systems, and Evaluations in Education, Riverside, California, 1972.* Austin, Texas: Dissemination Center for Bilingual Education, 1973.

[25] Kestelman, Maiztegui, and Lopez, *op. cit.*, p. 1.

Table 1. Programs for Initial Stages of Bilingual Instruction at
Elementary or Secondary Level

Initial Stage of Bilingual Instruction

Client	Program
Monolingual Spanish-speaker or nonEnglish-speaker (NES)	1. Concept acquisition, formation, and development must be in Spanish, that is, the medium of instruction is Spanish. 2. Reading or acquisition of literacy skills in Spanish. 3. ESL (English as a Second Language) instruction must take place in a very orderly, sequenced fashion so that the student masters English first in its oral form, then in its written form. Care must also be exercised so that the content of the curriculum is incorporated into the ESL lessons as the students acquire facility with English.
Client Monolingual English-speaker	**Program** 1. Concept acquisition, formation, and development in English (that is, the medium of instruction is English). 2. Reading or acquisition of initial literacy skills in English. 3. SSL (Spanish as a Second Language) instruction must be carefully planned and sequenced so that student masters Spanish first in its oral form, then in its written form. Attention should be given to incorporating the vocabulary and concepts of the regular academic program into the SSL program as mastery of Spanish proceeds.
Client Predominant English-speaker	**Program** 1. Concept acquisition, formation, and development in English, reinforced in Spanish. 2. Reading or acquisition of literacy skills done in English but reinforced in Spanish. 3. SSL (Spanish as a Second Language) instruction should continue since this is the weaker of the two languages. However, the SSL lessons at this stage of development should begin to reflect more and more the requirements of the regular academic program: vocabulary concepts, ideas, information.
Client Predominant Spanish-speaker or limited-English-speaker	**Program** 1. Concept acquisition, formation, and development in Spanish, reinforced in English. 2. Reading or acquisition of literacy skills should be done in English.

3. ESL (English as a Second Language) instruction should continue since English is the weaker language. At this stage, the regular academic program can begin to play a greater role in the ESL program. The ESL lesson can be designed based on the vocabulary, concepts, and information mandated by the academic program.

1. The alternate day approach—instruction is given in English one day and in Spanish the next.

2. The alternate discipline approach—instruction is given in Spanish in one subject and in English the next. Care should be taken that all subjects are taught in both languages at some time.

3. The alternate half-day approach—instruction is given half the day in English and half the day in Spanish. Again, all subjects should be taught in both languages at some time.

4. The alternate week approach—instruction is given entirely in Spanish one week and entirely in English the next.

5. Or, the student is totally immersed in one or the other language for six weeks at a time or even longer.

Whatever the approach, the goal of a maintenance program is to continue to develop and refine both languages so that students will become fully functional bilingual/bicultural individuals.

If, on the other hand, the philosophical considerations are more political or economic in nature, a shift or bridge program will take place. This transitional type of program places no great import on the native language of the nonEnglish-speaking child. The emphasis is on English acquisition and moving the child into the regular curriculum with all deliberate speed. In this case, the fact that the student has become bilingual and bicultural does not argue for maintaining a dual language instructional program. Such transitional programs are not favored by most bilingual education experts.

The Latino students' presence in America's schools is a visible reality. They bring with them a rich linguistic and cultural background which is an asset to the schools and communities of the nation. Latino students should be viewed as valuable resources rather than as problems in our educational institutions.

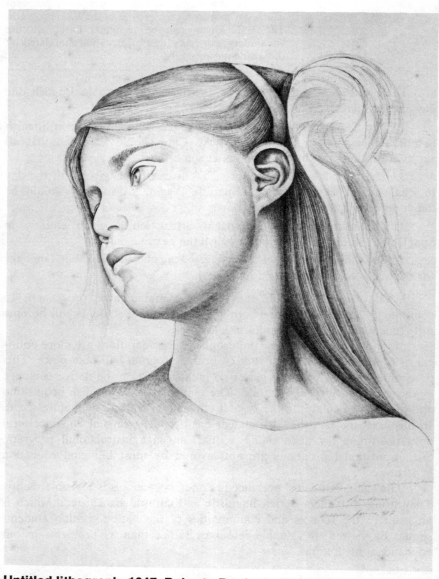

Untitled lithograph, 1947, Roberto Berdecio (Bolivia)
Courtesy of the Museum of Modern Art of Latin America
Washington, D.C.

2.
Curriculum Development
Rita M. Deyoe and Juan D. Solis

Bilingual education demands competent, serious curriculum study and development efforts for the same reasons monolingual education does. Some of the particular elements and priorities may differ from those of a monolingual curriculum, but bilingual learners differ more among themselves in needs, talents, and proficiencies than they differ as a group from monolingual learners. The reason for stating this obvious fact is that a good many educators and publishers ignore this rich intra-group diversity when selecting or developing bilingual curriculum. Just as is the case when educators sincerely and seriously attempt to educate *any* learners, bilingual learners' needs, preferences, and proficiencies must be observed, analyzed, and accommodated. Similarly, the attitudes of parents, administrators, and teachers who affect the implementation of the curriculum must also be accommodated. The attitudes of these adults have more influence on the students' perceptions of education than the quality or quantity of printed and audiovisual curriculum materials available.

This chapter incorporates the above orientation with the wealth of previous research and practice in curriculum development. This knowledge will be applied to the particular elements and priorities of bilingual education.

Criteria for Developing and Selecting Bilingual Curricula

Many of the criteria which apply to designing, developing, or selecting high quality bilingual materials do not differ from the criteria for monolingual materials. This section, therefore, will deal only with issues which are especially crucial in bilingual education. For more general types of criteria the reader is referred to the references at the end of this chapter.

17

Linguistic Criteria

There are five linguistic criteria which must be applied in selecting or developing bilingual curricula:

1. *Respect the "Whorfian hypothesis."* The research of Edward Sapir, as further developed by Benjamin Whorf, points to the observation that "the same words in another language" do not mean the same thing because language facilitates true communication only when the communicators also share a common culture.

Some implications of this principle would be that direct translation cannot produce authentic materials and that translated curricula cannot produce authentic coordinate bilinguals (those who have full command of two separate cultural-linguistic systems). Translated materials encourage compound bilingualism (using one set of structures with the vocabularies of two languages), which limits the learners' abilities to acquire appropriate idiomatic expressions needed to communicate in standard dialects of both languages. Language is an expression of culture and, as such, the validity of the content of a message is dependent on its being expressed via the language of the culture to which the content belongs.

2. *Avoid linguistic stereotyping.* Materials which depict those who speak with an accent as economically poor, uneducated, or less intelligent than others serve to stereotype bilinguals negatively and to contribute to the development of a negative self-image. Avoidance of linguistic stereotyping must always be the case even when the goal of the lesson is to contrast linguistic differences in two languages to assist the learner in acquiring standard pronunciation and grammar.

3. *Use local dialects, code-switching.* It is essential to select and develop materials which give value to regional, local, even personal usages of language which have meaning for the student. Also, it is crucial to provide opportunities for students to learn other regional varieties of language and to encourage mastery of some form of the international standard in each language. Otherwise, the student is not given an equal opportunity to acquire the skills needed for interaction and socioprofessional mobility outside a particular region. This does not mean the curriculum (or the teacher) should encourage the student to put aside all nonstandard forms, but rather that the learner should be encouraged to develop "code-switching" skills— the ability to select and use whichever variety of the language or languages will be the most effective, efficient, and expressive means of communication in a particular situation.

Most English-speakers do this often, sometimes unconsciously, as when a northerner who moves to the South begins to acquire a "drawl."

Sometimes code-switching occurs purposely, as when politicians affect the manner of speech of a special group or region in order to court the support of those they imitate by "honoring their language." In order to accomplish this goal of linguistic flexibility for bilingual learners, both the prepared curriculum and the teacher's implementation of it must honor the students' language. Such acceptance is required because it affects the learner's sense of pride in his or her identity.

4. *Respect language as communication rather than as a marker for social discrimination.* As models, both the prepared curriculum and the teacher's implementation of the learning should emphasize that all types of language are appropriate in some place at some time. The type of language used in a State of the Union message is just as inappropriate at the racetrack as street language would be in an international tariff agreement. However, speakers of *all* the varieties should respect the "rulers of the turf" on which they tread at a given moment and should make a sincere attempt to master the code which permits the most effective communication. Both teachers and materials should be sufficiently flexible to include the necessary accommodations. When the class lesson deals with events of general, national, or international interest, the most acceptable medium of communication is a standard variety of a language of wider communication. When the content of the class deals with experience, interpretation, or events in a particular locale or region, the most acceptable language is the variety of language appropriate to the setting, including the learning of whatever in-group expressions may be needed to ensure effective communication.

5. *Avoid placing bilingual learners in "double jeopardy" with respect to language proficiency.* It is important to arrive at a measure for the appropriate levels of language proficiency expected of bilingual learners. However, adding all the proficiency in English expected of English monolinguals to all the proficiency in Spanish expected of Spanish monolinguals will not be an appropriate set of expectations for Spanish-English bilinguals. The nature of bilingualism is such that the bilingual's learning will exceed that of the monolingual in aspects not measured by tests designed to assess the limited kinds of learning accomplished through a unilingual medium. Likewise, so long as sociolinguistic discrimination continues in this country, the levels and types of achievement of English-speakers who learn a second language voluntarily are likely to vary in emphasis and content from non-English-speakers who are obliged to learn English as a prerequisite to economic survival. The finer points of style and expression in a language are naturally intriguing to those who study language as a refined hobby. They hardly form an appropriate measure for the achievement of those who

learn two languages because each is a necessary medium of basic communication for social and economic survival. Thus to measure bilingual learners by monolingual standards is to place them in double jeopardy.

No valid conclusions as to the language achievement of bilinguals can be drawn from monolingual measures. As an example, consider the instruments used to determine the difficulty of reading materials in English which often rely on word length as an indicator of difficulty. They are based on the assumption that Anglo-Saxon terms (which are predominantly one-syllable words) are easier to learn. However, for the bilingual learner whose first language is Spanish, French, Portuguese, or Italian, the two or three syllable latinate terms will often be easier to learn because they are cognates of words he or she already knows. Thus, an English book that represents a third grade level challenge for a monolingual English-speaker may be much easier for a Spanish-English bilingual than the so-called primer which contains an almost exclusively Anglo-Saxon vocabulary.

Cultural Content Criteria

1. *Choose evolving cultural representations, not picturesque traditionalism.* While it is important for bilingual learners to develop a sense of identity and continuity with their cultural heritage, it is a flagrant violation of students' civil rights to ask them to conserve a negative interpretation of their heritage. Often even programs dedicated to liberating Latinos from poverty, oppression, and discrimination emphasize the domestic role of Latinos to the exclusion of their participation as equals in the social and economic affairs of this nation. If such attitudes appear in curricula intended to promote the upward mobility of Latinos it is unfortunate indeed, for they exemplify the flaunting of efforts at curriculum reforms.

Likewise, customs related to religion, family, and community must be represented as evolving aspects of culture which grow, change, and become more varied in a very mobile, industrial society. To focus on a simplistic, traditional, rural social organization as the ideal of Latino culture is to deprive bilingual learners of opportunities to analyze and adjust to the modern urban society in which most of them now live. If students sense too great a disparity between the cultural and social ideals presented in the curriculum and the realities of their own lives, they may reject the curriculum, their heritage, and, consequently, a part of themselves. Cultural content in the curriculum which leads learners to view themselves as inadequate cannot contribute to the development of a positive self-image or a well-integrated personality. In short, the picturesque traditionalism of the past should be presented as part of the past rather than as an ideal for the present or future.

2. *Distinguish between cultural expression and sociopolitical experience and reaction.* In many bilingual curricula, the pertinent information about Latinos which has been omitted in the past from the Anglo-oriented "mainstream" curriculum has been lumped together under the rubric of "culture." This is valid from an anthropological viewpoint since culture includes all aspects of the life of a particular group. However, from a curriculum design and implementation perspective, this way of dealing with culture reinforces discrimination in the mainstream curriculum and promotes confusion in the bilingual curriculum. Cultural expression through music, dance, crafts, costume, cuisine, myths, legends, and religion forms a fascinating group of topics to investigate, experience, and enjoy. For bilingual learners it is a means of "touching" their ethnic heritage, and for monolingual learners it is an opportunity to expand their horizons and acquire an increasingly global and cosmopolitan perspective.

On the other hand, the contributions of Latino leaders to the politics, economics, social progress, and national history of the United States and other nations is important for *all* students to learn as part of a common multicultural national history. Thomas Paine and César Chávez are leaders who have vitally affected the lives of all Americans and the study of their contributions should not be segregated into Anglo Social Studies vs. Chicano Social Studies. In the long run, Latinos will benefit far more by having all students understand and appreciate César Chávez's and Dolores Huerta's contributions to this nation as a whole than by merely having their pictures placed on bulletin boards in segregated bilingual classrooms.

In short, developing and selecting curriculum to assure equal access to society's benefits for bilinguals in the United States cannot be limited to the curricula for *bilingual* learners. Further polarizing the knowledge and experience of ethnic groups in the schools can hardly be expected to promote increased understanding and appreciation of the groups for each others' needs, rights, and contributions.

3. *Preserve and promote cultural values which promote group and individual growth, expression, and well-being.* One of the advantages of being a multicultural nation is having the opportunity to analyze, compare, and synthesize a set of social values which selects the healthiest, most positive values from each of many cultures and recombines them to produce a rational, yet sensitive, response to the needs of this pluralistic society. Just as the excessive paternalism of many traditional societies limits the growth and development of the individual, the excessive competition of modern industrial society is destructive to social relationships and serves to promote alienation, conflict, and violence.

All curricula, but especially bilingual curricula, should stress the fact that in each culture, as in each person, there are positive and negative characteristics and that a multicultural nation has the same advantage as the multifaceted person, that of promoting the most positive values of each group or facet. It is important to ensure that curriculum materials represent the result of this analysis and comparison of cultural values as being a synthesis of the best of many worlds rather than as a simplistic choice in favor of one ethnic orientation over another. Realistically, no such clearcut choice occurs; even the most insular Anglo monolingual eats tacos and burritos and dances to "black" music and even the most radical Chicano drinks coke and dances to corridos Norteños which were produced by the synthesis of German, Polish, Scottish, Spanish, and native American musical traditions, rhythms, and instruments.

4. *Distinguish between positive cultural developments and the effects of the "culture of poverty, oppression, and discrimination."* Often the studies of sociologists identify certain sets of values as characteristic of a particular ethnic group. However, many such studies actually document the frequency and intensity of poverty, political oppression, and social discrimination experienced by an easily identifiable minority group. For example, a common set of cultural values which are ascribed to Latinos are these: traditionalism, familism, paternalism, personalism, fatalism, and "machismo" (cf. Andersson and Boyer).[1] However, if one observes any of several rural, impoverished communities whose members are easily identifiable by their physical appearance or language usage, these same characteristics tend to be observed in excess. It should be noted that the majority culture sees these characteristics as positive when ascribed in moderate quantity and quality to middle-class Anglo monolinguals. However, when the same characteristics are observed among impoverished rural people in Appalachia, in black urban ghettos, or in rural or urban Latino communities, they become pathological symptoms of minority culture. Latinos are led to conclude that when they try too hard to emulate the values of the majority and thus prepare themselves for upward mobility, the majority will devise a means of thwarting that threat to their monopolistic situation.

A brief discussion of machismo best illustrates our contention. The use of this term to denote exploitative, violent, sexist, male behavior has been promoted by English-speakers. To most Spanish-speakers machismo has more to do with courage, self-reliance, and the ability to be "tender yet tough" and "demanding but just" than it has to do with male supremacy and the exploitation of women as servants and sex objects. In point of fact,

---

[1] T. Andersson and M. Boyer. *Bilingual Schooling in the United States.* Volume II. Appendix K. Washington, D.C.: U.S. Government Printing Office, 1970.

most Spanish-speakers would regard a violent man who exploited women as the antithesis of the true "macho." Likewise, a woman who is noted for her courage, self-reliance, and ability to persevere toward noble goals is frequently referred to admiringly as being "muy macha," with no insinuation that she lacks femininity.

The reason for this lengthy discussion of what can or should be labeled Latino culture is that federal bilingual programs require the teaching of the nonEnglish-speaker's cultural heritage. Therefore, determining what constitutes culture is a crucial aspect of curriculum design, development, and selection for bilingual education. It is apparent that the right to appreciate and honor one's cultural heritage is crucial to the development of a positive self-concept and an integrated personality. Based on the preceding illustrations, it is equally apparent that the content that is presented as culture and the manner in which the cultural curriculum is implemented will determine whether past "sins of omission" are rectified or whether newer and more prejudicial "sins of commission" replace them.

5. *Demonstrate the value and relevance of the experience and knowledge of the learner's parents, relatives, and community.* Not only is it important that the students' parents, relatives, and friends not be excluded from the curriculum; it is equally essential that they be specifically included. In some cases it is important to work to improve the bilingual student's self-concept by improving the parents' self-image. All students need support and encouragement from their homes and communities to succeed in school. However, unless the families of bilingual learners are consulted, informed, and involved in the education of their children, it is difficult for them to provide adequate guidance and encouragement to their children. Parents who have input into the education of their child have a better concept of themselves as parents and are more likely to believe the child is able to succeed in school. This confidence is transferred to the learner who is then motivated to fulfill the expectations of his or her parents and the parents in turn feel they have an important role in their child's intellectual development. Therefore, bilingual curricula should be designed and developed or selected to provide structured roles for parent participation. Ideally, homework assignments frequently should involve having the learner seek information about practical applications of school learning in both the work and leisure activities of relatives and friends.

Methods and Learning Styles

1. *Cognitive process methods, the discovery approach, and other "democratic" learning techniques are important means of intellectual up-*

ward mobility and are less likely to be "culture-bound" than some other methods. Methodologies which teach the student to think and which respect the learner's observation, experience, and creativity need to be used with bilingual students to increase their self-confidence and positive self-image. Also, judicious use of so-called "discovery approaches" permits the teacher to find out how the students are actually interpreting the curriculum. However, until the students gain a measure of self-confidence, teachers who implement open-ended learning techniques in a bilingual setting should be reminded to provide large amounts of verbal and nonverbal encouragement, to avoid embarrassing or ridiculing students who seem timid, and to utilize small groups and peer-pairs. These techniques should be tried before asking for individual responses or calling on particular students. When individual responses are desired, it is usually preferable to indicate to the students that they will all be asked to participate, but the teacher should remain flexible as to the order in which students are called upon. A student who seems afraid or unwilling to respond the first time he or she is called on should not be reprimanded. This is tantamount to "losing face before the community" and will often result in greater timidity and reticence in the future.

In general, because of the competitive achievement values which prevail in Anglo society, getting mainstream students to work alone and volunteer their own ideas is not usually difficult. Most Latino cultures place more value on being well thought of by one's peers than on showing off one's own talents. In fact, the latter is usually viewed as bad manners. Therefore, if the Latino child is to acquire the self-reliance and outspokenness valued by the majority society without denying his or her own cultural values, the experience will be least upsetting and most successful if it is structured so that all the students contribute and receive positive reinforcement, but no one student receives either excessive praise or particular blame.

The cognitive process orientation aligns itself closely with the goal of producing independent "self-starters" who strive and achieve with little or no external guidance or motivation. This is a desirable aspect of biculturalism for all Latino children as it prepares them to compete and survive in the mainstream work economy. However, it should not be attained at the expense of the positive aspects of Latino cultures which value the harmony and respect of one's peers above selfish ambitions.

2. *Behavior modification, programmed learning, and other authoritarian methods and techniques can be used effectively to teach certain kinds of skills and information.* Various kinds of programmed learning and intensive skill practice and drill are useful in teaching specific information which

needs to be memorized or skills which need to be internalized until they become automatic. However, such learning must be perceived as purposeful, meaningful, and useful or it will be forgotten. These statements are true for students in general but they have special relevance in selecting and designing curricula for Latino students. In particular, language learning requires the internalization of rules and the memorization of vocabulary. Unless the rules are used and unless the vocabulary is meaningful to the student, the noncreative language skills which can be taught so efficiently by programmed and mechanical means are liable to be forgotten far more rapidly than they were learned. Furthermore, if such materials have not been enhanced with creative applications to meaningful situations, the bilingual child is left with little more than a certificate indicating several years of obedient busywork.

The reason busywork is such a frequent occurrence in the school life of Latino children is that they are taught to respect authority, conditioning them to be compliant recipients of highly structured, semi-mechanical, anti-creative curricula. Such curricula are often recommended as being ideal for use with Latino students because they are "easy for the teacher and the students respond very well." The fallacy in this recommendation is that it overlooks a crucial question: What are the children being taught to prepare for? Unless the programmed learning is complemented by creative applications of the skills acquired, the students are being trained to be compliant robots who perform specific tasks according to particular requirements. This is certainly part of the world of work in an industrial society; however, when it is the only method used for an entire group of students, alike only in home language and culture, it constitutes ethnic imperialism and deprives bilingual students of the opportunity to prepare themselves as independent thinkers, leaders, or professionals in fields which require creative thinking and decision-making. Thus, programmed learning should be used for specific memorization and skills learning, but it should *not* be used where more democratic methods are available, even if the democratic methods require more effort from both the teacher and the students.

Another consideration in forming an eclectic methodology for bilingual curricula is the concern of the majority society with respect to whether bilingual education is working or not. To those who observe elite families throughout the world paying outrageous tuition fees for their children in private bilingual schools, asking whether bilingual education works is rather like asking whether a Mercedes-Benz is a good make of automobile. However, because of the considerable longing some people have to prove bilingual education ineffective, educators are urged to employ curricula which will show results fast. This means there is pressure, from both those who wish bilingual education to fail and those who know it can succeed, to have analyzable data which document the learning of bilingual students.

The experience-oriented discovery approach may promote learning which will be useful throughout the rest of the life of the learner. This is hardly convenient for those who want to prove the success or failure of bilingual education on the basis of six months to two years of partial program implementation. The curricula which facilitate such measures are those which concentrate on memorization and other low level cognitive domain types of learning that are easily tested with computer-scored objective tests. Such curricula can be evaluated as succeeding or failing by checking skills in the use of verb forms and arithmetic operations but such test results indicate very little about why some students quit school in junior high and why some of those who scored high on the tests cannot balance a checkbook and why some who scored low are running for Congress.

3. *All students need practice in both "field dependent" and "field independent" cognitive styles.* This is merely a direct statement of what has been discussed earlier in regard to the relative value of cognitive process versus programmed learning methods. According to most of the research, "field independent" learners are more likely to be monolingual Anglo males than women or minority group males. Thus it is tempting to assume that there may be some relationship between cognitive style and political and economic opportunity and power. However, employment studies also indicate that the most frequent reason people lose jobs is that they have personality conflicts with their superiors. So, as was suggested before, it is not enough to accommodate the learner's most natural cognitive style. If Latinos are to have equal access to the benefits of the mainstream economy, they must master both cognitive styles and learn to utilize the appropriate style in the appropriate situation.

4. *All students need experience working alone, with a partner, and in groups.* Many Latino children (and adults) prefer working with a partner or in a group to working alone. However, the bilingual person who wishes to succeed in the economic mainstream in the United States must also be willing and able to work alone and to take individual responsibility for tasks and decisions. Likewise, many Anglos need to learn how to work with others in a cooperative, rather than a competitive mode. Bilingual curricula should make provisions for a wide variety of individual, peer-pair, and group learning activities. Any curriculum which restricts learners to one pattern of human interaction fails to prepare the students for the diverse situations they will find in the world of business and family life.

5. *Social pluralism is a necessary curriculum orientation in both bilingual and monolingual materials.* First, it is appropriate to define the term we have coined. Social pluralism is the positive promotion of diversity in the roles of people—to combat racism, ethnocentrism, and elitism, as well as sexism, agism, and discrimination on the basis of physical handicaps, academic experience, or marital status. Thus, bilingual curricula should not exclude the contributions of non-Latinos (unless complemented by other multicultural curricula for the same students). Sexism in bilingual materials is as much a violation of the rights of learners as sexism in monolingual curricula. "White racism" in monolingual curricula cannot be combated with "brown racism" in bilingual curricula. The only viable alternative is the elimination of racism in both monolingual and bilingual materials. Racism in any curriculum materials infringes on the rights of the groups that are discriminated against since the omission of information or the misinformation given will affect the learner's attitudes toward people of other races.

Readability, Vocabulary, and Style

1. *Readable₁ is not Readable₂.* The vocabulary that is easiest for a Spanish-English bilingual will differ from that which is easiest for a Spanish-speaking monolingual (in Spanish) and it will differ from that which is easiest for an English-speaking monolingual (in English). In general, for a U.S. bilingual, English latinate cognates of Spanish words will be easier than the corresponding Anglo-Saxon term (for example, comprehend vs. understand). Spanish borrowings or coinages related to the English word for concrete objects and verbs will be preferred in Spanish ("estufa" vs. "fogón," "rentar" vs. "arrendar" or "alquilar"). However, this varies tremendously from one Latino group to another and from one region to another. This is one of the reasons the "language experience" approach to teaching beginning language arts has become very popular. When language usage varies so greatly, the best source of curriculum content for beginning language arts is the learner. However, this should not continue to be the *only* source. In order to maximize the advantage of being bilingual the students must learn to deal with more than one variety in each language.

2. *Vocabulary is used for communication.* That words are used to convey meaning seems to be an obvious conclusion; however, some vocabulary lists are based on the statistical frequency of the occurrence of the same word in adult speech or in adult writing. Vocabulary selected for teaching children oral communication or literacy should consist of words which are useful for children to communicate their feelings, experiences,

and observations from a child's perspective. Again, the primary source of this vocabulary is the child. The topics overheard during free time, recess, or lunch time will provide a far more productive and meaningful basis for vocabulary selection and development than the word lists selected by a computer.

3. *Style is a product of experience, modeling, and experimentation.* The preferred style for general written and spoken English among monolinguals tends to be brief, blunt, and contemporary, with more verbs than adjectives. The preferred style for written and spoken Spanish among monolinguals is involved, intricate, detailed, and descriptive, with an emphasis on the courteously indirect expression. Most bilingual people alternate between these styles and combine them in highly individualistic ways. Bilingual learners may find the preferred English standard for style "blunt and cold," and they may react to the international standard Spanish style as too involved and hard to follow. In selecting and developing curricula for United States bilingual learners, it is appropriate to accommodate the students' preferences initially and later to introduce them to the standard literary styles of each language gradually. As in matters of readability and vocabulary, it is best to start with materials written in a style resembling that of the learner and to gradually introduce styles from other regions so that the student can acquire the skills of the languages of wider communication without losing the unique style of his or her own region.

This concludes the general discussion of some criteria for designing, developing, and selecting bilingual curricula which can be expected (a) to contribute to the establishment of learning environments and (b) to help equalize opportunities for Latino students to succeed in school and in the mainstream work economy of this country. The section which follows analyzes and evaluates the types of bilingual curricula currently available or under development and comments on the extent to which these materials are likely to be relevant, appropriate, or useful for U.S. Latino bilinguals.

A Taxonomy of Bilingual Curriculum Materials: Some Inherent Advantages and Disadvantages

It is important to clarify that this brief taxonomy covers the major types of materials that are being advertised for use in bilingual education programs in the United States, whether or not the materials were designed for that target population.

Monolingual English Materials

These are of two general types: materials which assume the learner is fluent in English, and those which assume the learner knows virtually no English.

1. *English for Native Speakers.* These are materials developed for monolingual (usually monocultural) United States or British children, and they are used with Latinos who are English dominant or for whom neither English as a Second Language (ESL) nor bilingual instruction is being provided.

Disadvantages: These materials are often monocultural or stereotypic in content. Linguistically, they offer no assistance to the bilingual learner in contrasting and comparing the two language systems, and they often emphasize types of word attack skills and structural analysis which are only relevant for monolingual learners.

Advantages: To the extent that any benefit can be gained from these materials by the bilingual learner, it probably lies in having been exposed to the same vocabulary and structures as the monolingual students. To the extent the materials are monocultural and stereotypic they initiate the bilingual learner into the majority culture's biased perception of the world.

It should be noted that several of the major publishing houses have drastically revised their monolingual materials to at least make the illustrations and some of the content multicultural.

2. *English for Speakers of Other Languages.* Most of these materials were originally developed for markets outside the United States. In many cases the original target population consisted of adults or secondary school students.

Disadvantages: Frequently, the content of these materials is directed toward the interests of adults or adolescents who have no contact with U.S. culture or the English language outside the classroom. United States bilinguals who need the beginning materials, however, are of a different age group. Materials written in the United States tend to be carefully controlled in terms of structure and vocabulary, but rather boring and mechanical in method. British materials, on the other hand, tend to utilize more stimulating and creative types of techniques but vocabulary and structural complexity often are virtually uncontrolled.

Advantages: The major advantage of these types of curricula is that they are often based on a careful analysis of contrasting linguistic and cultural patterns and are therefore much more appropriate and efficient for bilingual learners whose primary goal is mastery of the basic elements of the English language.

Monolingual Spanish Materials

These are of two general types: materials which assume the learner is fluent in Spanish (and lives in a particular Spanish-speaking country), and those which assume the student knows virtually no Spanish. There are also a few which assume the learner knows a particular regional version of Spanish and wishes to learn a dialect of wider communication.

1. *Spanish for Native Speakers.* These materials have been developed in one of the several Spanish-speaking nations for use with monolingual students who are essentially monocultural and who are expected to master an accepted national standard for language usage along with acquiring a knowledge of the literature of that nation in particular. Excerpts from the writing of notable authors from other Spanish-speaking nations and some English, German, Russian, and French writers whose works have been translated into Spanish are also usually included in these materials.

Disadvantages: The major problem with these materials is that they assume the student is fully prepared to deal with the large vocabulary and complex structures of academic Spanish. They also assume the learner is monolingual and provide no assistance in contrasting the rules of spelling, grammar, and pronunciation in the two languages. Most such materials are monocultural and exhibit considerable regional ethnocentrism. Many examples and cultural or historical references belong to the particular region and are not known to U.S. bilinguals.

Advantages: The advantages these materials can offer are those of exposure to Spanish as a language of wider communication, exposure to some common aspects of all Spanish-speaking cultures, and increased awareness of the diversity of culture and language among the world's Spanish-speakers.

2. *Spanish for English-Speakers.* These are materials developed in the United States to teach monolingual English-speaking high school and college students international standard Spanish.

Disadvantages: Usually the content of the lessons is directed toward the interests of adults or adolescents who have no contact with Spanish-speakers outside the classroom and whose major motive for learning Spanish may be to facilitate travel as a tourist in Spanish-speaking countries or to read literary works in Spanish. Thus, the purpose of the language study and the age level intended both differ from those of U.S. bilinguals who need beginning materials. Furthermore, these materials assume the learner is already literate and fluent in English at a high level of sophistication.

Advantages: The only advantage these materials offer is that they are often based on a contrastive analysis of the sounds, spelling, and grammar of the two languages.

3. *Spanish for Bilinguals.* A few such materials have been produced for use with Latino high school and college students.

Disadvantages: Most attempts of this sort are tremendously ethnocentric and admonish the student to learn traditional or "correct" Spanish rather than reinforcing the learner's own usage while providing practice in a dialect of wider communication. Also, such materials are prepared for adults and the content is outside the interest and vocabulary range of younger students.

Advantages: These materials do address the needs of U.S. bilinguals for curricula which contrast English and Spanish as well as contrasting regional usages of Spanish with the international standard.

Bilingual Materials Produced by Translating or Adapting From One Language to the Other

Most of the materials currently in development are produced in this way. Using this approach, the curriculum retains whatever advantages and disadvantages the original version had plus two important additional disadvantages.

Disadvantages: The particular cultural-linguistic disadvantage of translated materials is that even the most carefully adapted material is an attempt to express the realities of one culture in the words of another. This does a disservice to both and excludes the legitimate cultural expression of the second language. The methodological error of translating materials for bilingual learners is that it deprives them of the best motivation for learning the second language—a desire to understand materials not available in the first language.

Advantages: The two major advantages of these materials are that they are usually written for U.S. bilinguals of appropriate ages, and they may provide learners with curricula similar to those of their monolingual peers.

Bilingual Materials with Independent Cultural-Linguistic Strands

This method of bilingual curriculum design and development consists of preparing a common scope and sequence of behavioral objectives which are then developed independently in each language via comparable, but not identical, learning activities. The advantages of this approach are numerous:

1. The full range of learning objectives is available to each student through a language in which she or he may be expected to comprehend

fully and authentically the meaning of the concepts presented. Each student, therefore, has an opportunity to experience intellectual growth and academic success.

2. The specific content and learning methods are not repeated in the two language versions; therefore, new material is available to motivate the students to use their second language *within an authentic cultural frame of reference*. This provides for a realistic approach to producing behavior that is truly bicultural as well as bilingual and that allows the students to succeed in establishing meaningful, productive roles and relationships for themselves in both the minority and mainstream cultures. Only when this is accomplished will bilingual learners experience the feeling of a fully integrated self-image that will provide the self-confidence and emotional security essential to achievement in a multicultural United States society.

3. Because the content and activities vary in the two language versions, reinforcement activities are automatically provided that give additional practice to the bilingual learners. Such activities allow them to learn needed concepts and attitudes in a second language without the stigma of remedial work or oversimplified content.

4. This approach reflects the successful experiences of bilingual schools in many nations that present learners with the best and most authentic materials in each language, selected to fulfill the requirements of vigorous and demanding "baseline" objectives, and designed to respond to the students' entry level skills.

The best materials of this type are being developed to include the language and cultural experiences of several major groups of U.S. Spanish-speakers. With such materials, U.S. Latinos can hope to benefit from the advantages of coordinate bilingualism and biculturalism.

This is not to say that this type of bilingual curricula is the only kind that needs to be used. Ideally, it is the best kind of curriculum for initial teaching. However, more advanced students should have experience with both English for Native Speakers and Spanish for Native Speakers. Furthermore, teachers should use both English for Speakers of Other Languages and Spanish for English-Speakers curricula along with Spanish for Bilinguals materials to review and reinforce the full acquisition of English and Spanish as separate systems.

With respect to bilingual instruction in the content areas, the materials which are being prepared by the translation-adaptation process will assist the recent immigrant as will the content area materials prepared in other Spanish-speaking countries. However, for second and third generation Hispanic Americans, fully appropriate curricula in the content areas will not be available until they have been developed for U.S. bilinguals in both languages without resorting to translation. This is especially true in language arts and social sciences although it is also true in the areas of mathematics and science.

It is to be hoped that present and future attempts to develop appropriate materials for U.S. bilinguals may thrive and find prompt and efficient implementation in the classroom. In order for this to occur, bilingual teacher education must prepare teachers to select and implement appropriate curricula in a thorough and competent fashion.

References

T. Andersson and M. Boyer. *Bilingual Schooling in the United States.* Appendix K of Volume II. Washington, D.C.: U.S. Government Printing Office, 1970.

Marcia Baghban. *Como ayudar a su hijo a aprender ingles como segunda lengua.* Rita M. Deyoe and Ricardo L. Garcia, translators. Newark, Delaware: International Reading Association, 1975. (Micromonograph.)

Charles W. Beegle and Roy A. Edelfelt, editors. *Staff Development: Staff Liberation.* Washington, D.C.: Association for Supervision and Curriculum Development, 1977.

Louise M. Berman and Jessie A. Roderick, editors. *Feeling, Valuing, and the Art of Growing: Insights into the Affective.* Washington, D.C.: Association for Supervision and Curriculum Development, 1977.

Jerome S. Bruner. *The Process of Education.* Cambridge: Harvard University Press, 1975. 13th printing.

Martin Carnoy and Henry M. Levin. *The Limits of Educational Reform.* New York: David McKay Company, Inc., 1976.

O. L. Davis, Jr., editor. *Perspectives on Curriculum Development 1776-1976.* Washington, D.C.: Association for Supervision and Curriculum Development, 1976.

John Dewey. *Experience and Education.* New York: Collier Books, 1963.

Rita M. Deyoe. "To Alter the Message of the Schools: A Model of the Hidden Curriculum." *Scholar and Educator,* Summer/Fall 1977.

Rita M. Deyoe. "Theory as Practice in Multicultural Education." *Educational Horizons* 55(4); Summer 1977.

Ronald C. Doll. *Curriculum Improvement.* Boston: Allyn and Bacon, Inc., 1970. Second edition.

James Eaton. *An ABC of the Curriculum.* Edinburgh: Oliver and Boyd, 1975.

Educational Leadership. Washington, D.C.: Association for Supervision and Curriculum Development.

Elliot W. Eisner and Elizabeth Vallance, editors. *Conflicting Conceptions of Curriculum.* Berkeley: McCutchan Publishing Corporation, 1974.

ELT: English Language Teaching Journal. Neadsen, London, England: Oxford University Press.

EPIE Report, Number 73. *Selector's Guide for Bilingual Education Materials.* Volume 1, Spanish Language Arts. New York: EPIE Institute, 1976.

EPIE Report, Number 74. *Selector's Guide for Bilingual Education Materials.* Volume 2, Spanish "Branch" Programs. New York: EPIE Institute, 1976.

Paulo Freire. *Education for Critical Consciousness*. New York: The Seaburg Press, 1973.

Paulo Friere. *Pedagogy of the Oppressed*. Myra Bergman Ramos, translator. New York: The Seaburg Press, 1970.

Ricardo L. García. *Learning in Two Languages*. Bloomington, Indiana: Phi Delta Kappa Educational Foundation, 1976.

Ricardo L. García. *Enseñanza Bilingüe*. Bloomington, Indiana: Phi Delta Kappa Educational Foundation, 1976.

Carl A. Grant, editor. *Multicultural Education: Commitments, Issues, and Applications*. Washington, D.C.: Association for Supervision and Curriculum Development, 1977.

Harvard Educational Review. Volume 47. Longfellow Hall, Cambridge, Massachusetts: Harvard University Press.

Interracial Books for Children Bulletin. New York: Council on Interracial Books for Children, Inc.

Gary D. Keller, Richard V. Teschner, and Silvia Viera, editors. *Bilingualism in the Bicentennial and Beyond*. Jamaica, New York: Bilingual Press, 1976.

Francis Willard von Maltitz. *Living and Learning in Two Languages: Bilingual-Bicultural Education in the United States*. New York: McGraw-Hill Book Co., 1975.

Alex Molnar and John A. Zahorik, editors. *Curriculum Theory*. Washington, D.C.: Association for Supervision and Curriculum Development, 1977.

NABE, The Journal of the National Association for Bilingual Education. Volume 1, Numbers 1, 2, 3.

J. Abner Peddiwell. *The Saber-Tooth Curriculum*. New York: McGraw-Hill Book Company, Inc., 1939.

William Pinar, editor. *Heightened Consciousness, Cultural Revolution, and Curriculum Theory*. Berkeley: McCutchan Publishing Corporation, 1974.

Manuel Ramírez and Alfredo Castañeda. *Cultural Democracy, Bicognitive Development, and Education*. New York: Academic Press, Inc., 1974.

Manuel Ramírez, III, and Douglass R. Price-Williams. "Cognitive Styles of Children of Three Ethnic Groups in the United States." *Journal of Cross-Cultural Psychology* 5(2); June 1974.

Louis Rubin, editor. *The Future of Education: Perspectives on Tomorrow's Schools*. Boston: Allyn and Bacon, Inc., 1975.

Muriel Saville-Troike. *Foundations for Teaching English as a Second Language*. Englewood Cliffs, New Jersey: Prentice-Hall, Inc., 1976.

Jon Schaffarzick and David H. Hampson, editors. *Strategies for Curriculum Development*. Berkeley: McCutchan Publishing Corp., 1975.

Joseph J. Schwab and William R. Harper. *The Practical: A Language for Curriculum*. Washington, D.C.: National Education Association, 1970.

Antonio Simões, Jr., editor. *The Bilingual Child*. New York: Academic Press, 1976.

Richard V. Teschner, Garland D. Bills, and Jerry R. Craddock, editors. *The Spanish and English of United States Hispanos*. Arlington, Virginia: Center for Applied Linguistics, 1975.

TESOL Quarterly. 455 Nevils Building, Georgetown University, Washington, D.C.

Eleanor Wall Thonis. *Teaching Reading to Non-English Speakers*. New York: Collier Macmillan International, Inc., 1976.

Louise L. Tyler. *A Selected Guide to Curriculum Literature: An Annotated Bibliography*. Washington, D.C.: National Education Association, 1970.

3.
Language Assessment and Evaluation
Henry T. Trueba and Kamal K. Sridhar

One of the most recent and important developments in American education is its broadening acceptance of bilingualism. The "melting pot" theory of assimilation is starting to give way to the acceptance of linguistic diversity and cultural pluralism. Language loyalty, as is evidenced by the fact that linguistic minorities in the United States have maintained their native language and culture (Fishman, 1966), is recognized, accepted, and encouraged. This acceptance and encouragement has been expressed in two types of legislation: "The Bilingual Education Act of 1968, empowering Congress to appropriate funds for bilingual education projects; and legal provision in the schools of some states legitimizing languages other than English as the language of instruction in schools" (Kloss, 1971).

Several studies have been done in the past that trace the development, the current status, and the problems encountered by bilingual education programs: Andersson and Boyer (1970), Gaarder (1970), John and Horner (1971), Gonzales (1975), and Trueba (1976), to mention just a few.

On the one hand, since bilingual education as designed by legislators is a compensatory instrument to provide equal educational opportunities to limited English-speaking ability (L.E.S.A.) children, it is of paramount importance to assess the language proficiency of these children. And, on the other hand, since supporters of bilingual-bicultural education would hope to maintain the children's native language while providing them with ample opportunity to learn English as a second language, it is equally important to evaluate the effectiveness of bilingual instruction to accomplish native language maintenance and second language acquisition. Furthermore, the selection and placement of children in bilingual programs must be done according to criteria based not only on language proficiency but

35

also on language dominance. Therefore, it is necessary to test a child's language dominance.

This chapter will deal with the recent trends and developments in the area of language testing and evaluation with special reference to bilingual education. The chapter will include: (a) A description and discussion of existing tests that are commonly used for assessing the language competence of bilingual students. The tests cover such broad areas as language proficiency, dominance, comprehension, and oral skills. Some of the tests included in this discussion are the Bilingual Syntax Measure; Short Tests of Linguistic Skills; Ilyin Oral Interview; Dos Amigos Verbal Language Scales; Tests for Auditory Comprehension of Language, English/Spanish; and Oral Language Evaluation. (b) A discussion of the well-known phenomenon of test bias, the kinds of cross-cultural biases that exist, the identification of biases in language assessment instruments, biases that exist in testing procedures, in grading, and in the examiners themselves. (c) Alternatives that would minimize the effect of competition and biases, one alternative being criterion-referenced testing. The merits and demerits of norm-referenced and criterion-referenced testing procedures will be discussed from the point of view of language assessment and placement in bilingual education programs. Finally, (d) a brief discussion of the legal implications of current student testing practices, followed by a short summary and conclusion.

Language Testing Instruments

Until fairly recently, language tests were usually achievement tests, evaluating students' language performance in terms of the content they had been exposed to in the classrooms. Currently, the emphasis is more on aptitude, a student's ability to learn the language and thereby function effectively in the context of a given language. This has come about partly as a result of the current emphasis on communicative competence as the ultimate goal of all language instruction, and partly in response to the demands of the federal legislation that asks for tests which predict accurately a child's ability to use a language effectively in day-to-day classroom interactions. This shift of emphasis in the functional use of language is apparent in the Bilingual Syntax Measure.

The Bilingual Syntax Measure (BSM)

The Bilingual Syntax Measure by Marina K. Burt, Heidi C. Dulay, and E. Hernandez-Chavez has been developed after a great deal of research in the area of child language acquisition. It is a refined instrument designed to measure the student's acquisition of grammatical structures in English and Spanish, to be used essentially in the primary grades K-3. The BSM is an oral instrument which uses illustrations that are within a child's frame of reference, and thus elicits natural speech samples. The principle behind the development of the BSM is that it avoids the drawbacks of traditional vocabulary tests that are culturally biased in the sense that these tests are dominated by vocabulary items from the dominant white middle-class culture. Also, as the manual points out, the BSM does not take into account pronunciation, which again varies considerably from one social class to another and from region to region. Thus, syntax is the only area that is selected by the BSM. The following key generalizations from research in psycholinguistics helped in the development of the BSM:

1. Children acquire certain syntactic structures in a systematic manner as they progress through successive stages of language acquisition.

2. The acquisition of these syntactic structures in an ordered and systematic manner applies to second language as well as to first language learners, although the acquisition order for first and second language learners differs in some respects.

3. Children do not typically transfer the syntactic rules of their native language to a second language when their linguistic environment includes peer speech in the target language; instead, children of diverse language backgrounds will follow a similar progression in learning a second language.

The BSM does not claim to measure the student's actual dominance, but an approximation in each of the following categories. The categories and the corresponding ranges of the Syntax Acquisition Index (SAI) are:

1 = Proficient (95-100)
2 = Intermediate (85-94)
3 = Survival (45-84)
4 = Non-speaking (below 44).

Another interesting feature of the BSM is that it gives explicit criteria for assigning points, and gives a wide range of scores especially for those in the "non-speaking" category: 0 points—no structure ("two child"); 1 point—misformed structure ("two childs"); 2 points—correct structure ("two children").

Thus, the misforming or overgeneralization of rules is taken into account, and the child is not penalized for overgeneralization, a salient feature in child language acquisition (Brown, 1973). It is considered language proficiency in progress. Also, "non-speaking" levels at which the student understands some vocabulary and syntax in the target language (non-native language) but cannot produce it is also documented via the BSM. Some instruments ignore this category altogether. The BSM seems to be a promising instrument, and in the years to come it may be able to supply all the much needed data in the areas of validity and reliability. For a detailed review of the test, see Oller (1976).

Short Test of Linguistic Skills (STLS)

The Short Test of Linguistic Skills (STLS), developed by Charles K. Frederickson and John W. Wick, assesses the language dominance and the general achievement level of bilingual children, especially those between seven and 15 years of age (roughly 2nd through 8th grades). The test measures a student's competence in the four major linguistic areas: listening, speaking, reading, and writing. Each of these areas is divided into four parts, thus testing a student on a whole range of skills. Also, parallel forms of the test in languages such as Arabic, Chinese, Greek, Italian, Japanese, Korean, Filipino, Polish, Spanish, and Vietnamese are available to assess the language dominance of children from diverse ethnic backgrounds.

The test, as it now exists, has been much revised and scrutinized since the original pilot testing in 1974 and 1975. The STLS was normed in Chicago. It was hoped that the procedure used would enable the teachers to place children in different categories of language dominance based upon the child's absolute score on the English half of the test, and the child's score on the English half relative to his or her score on the other language half. The procedure to be followed involves a panel of experts to examine the test and determine three cutoff points: (a) The minimum number of items on the English test that a student must get correct in order to be rated "acceptable" in English; (b) the minimum number of items on the English test a child can get right before being considered fluent in English; and (c) the size of the discrepancy between the other language and English test scores beyond which a child is to be considered "other dominant." These cutoff points, it is hoped, aid in the classification of children into low, medium, or high fluency categories for both English and the native language, and in determining the dominant language of the child (Day, 1977).

There are no studies reported for validity checks or for reliability, nor are there any studies reported or data given to support the claim that the different language forms are parallel forms, equivalent in every respect. Also, there is practically no information given on how to interpret the scores or how to use the score in adapting and changing the curriculum to suit the individual child's needs. However, there is no doubt that an assessment instrument for use in large urban, cosmopolitan, and multilingual settings is very much needed, and the STLS was developed to meet this demand. But, it is far from complete. Intensive research is needed to make this test acceptable and effective, for in its existing state, it does not fulfill what it professes to do.

Ilyin Oral Interview (IOI)

Developed by Donna Ilyin, the Ilyin Oral Interview (IOI) was originally used for placement of adults into English as a Second Language (ESL) programs, giving them credit for comprehension and communication, without penalizing them for incorrect or unacceptable syntax. As the title suggests, it is an oral interview, emphasizing communicative abilities in speaking and understanding with no reading or writing. The interview is available in two forms: Bill and Tom. The test is based on a series of pictures which are all about the same person. Each picture has a clock showing the time, so that the examinee has to respond with the appropriate time or verb tense.

The manual recommends a two point scoring system:

0 = Information given is inappropriate or unintelligible (grammar and structure may or may not be correct).
1 = Information given is appropriate and intelligible (one or more mistakes in grammar or structure).
2 = Information given is appropriate and intelligible (no grammar or structure mistakes).

The progression of items from simple to more difficult in each form of the test is based on research involving item difficulty. This is a refreshing idea, and the author deserves credit for saving the non-native speaker of English from experiencing initial failure. Reliability figures on the experimental and first edition of the test range from .86 to .98. The 50 item test and the earlier 30 item version are the result of intensive item-analysis and item discrimination procedures used in field testing/experimental versions of the test. Detailed descriptions of the test, including the standard error of measurement for each of the four reference groups trying out the test are given. The four groups were: (a) 180 students in two adult center ESL programs in San Francisco, differing in language proficiency and education levels, ranging in age from 18 to 75; (b) French-speaking students in an intensive English program in Canada, ranging in age from 18 to 25, with three or more years of formal instruction in English; (c) foreign students in a California full-time intensive language training program, all secondary school graduates, varying in their background and exposure to English; and, (d) employees in a New York on-the-job upgrading program, including speakers of second dialects, with varied language backgrounds.

Ilyin cautions that the results are still tentative and should be considered so. The author also states that she is particularly interested in the correlation of IOI with other existing ESL tests. It would be interesting to see how the IOI correlates with other tests of oral language skills used specially in bilingual education programs. IOI, as it is, is certainly worth considering, for it is easy to administer and score, but its usefulness in bilingual education programs needs to be established before one can recommend it without any reservations.

Dos Amigos Verbal Language Scales

Dos Amigos Verbal Language Scales by Donald E. Critchlow, was developed to assess the language dominance in children for both English and Spanish, and to define the developmental levels for each child in both languages. In the words of the author, ". . . they [the tests] will assist the psychologist or special educator in evaluation of learning difficulties of the English/Spanish-speaking child" (Critchlow, 1974: 8). The test is to be used for children between the ages of 5 and 14. The test is administered individually and the examiner has to be bilingual. The test consists of two scales, consisting of 85 stimulus words for each language, arranged in a hierarchical manner, from easy to difficult. The examiner is supposed to continue until the child misses five words consecutively. The number of correct responses is to be recorded as the raw score, and the corresponding percentile score is given in the manual under "Age Table." The raw scores for the two languages help the examiner to determine the percentile scores for each child by consulting the appropriate Age Table. A comparison of the two percentages shows the dominant language of the child, the higher the percentile, the greater the dominance. The percentile indicates the individual child's level of language development as compared to a sample of other bilingual-bicultural children belonging to the same age group. The author recommends auditory and perception tests for children whose scores fall below the 50th percentile in both languages compared to their specific age group.

Test items reflect the samples of speech utterances in classrooms, kindergarten through grade six. Lists of frequently used words for each grade were compiled. How systematically the compilation was done is unknown. This test was one of the instruments that was used to evaluate 30 third and fourth graders who were identified as having reading problems.

The manual states that the Dos Amigos results correlated highly (positively) with the Gilmore Oral Reading Test. The test scores are not reported, neither are the correlations, which makes it frustrating and difficult for those who might want to consider this test for use in their classrooms. No reliability studies are given. It was, however, field tested with over 300 children who met either one or more of the following criteria: 1. Mexican American ancestry, 2. Spanish mother tongue, 3. Reared in a Mexican American cultural milieu.

The standardization group on which the normative data were based consisted of 1,224 children from South Texas, between the grade range of kindergarten and 6th grade.

Teschner (1977) reviewing the Dos Amigos comments that there are just three alternatives permitted for the 85 English selections, and seven for the Spanish list. Also, many of the stimulus words in both sections allow for more than one response. In the antonym section, ". . . *costly* can be 'inexpensive' as well as 'cheap', and for Spanish, *enfermo/sano* can also stimulate 'curado', 'mejorado', 'aliviado', or even 'bien' " (Teschner: 202). While expressing surprise at the fact that the educators had not spotted the possibility of multiple responses, Teschner is concerned that the Spanish dominance could be underestimated. This occurs only in the Spanish version of the test. He concludes with the suggestion that this test should be used carefully, by alert bilingual examiners who are willing to accept a whole array of antonyms that are beyond the responses cited by Critchlow. (Teschner, 1977:203). One also wonders if this could be a test more appropriate for students living in South Texas (as normative data were collected there), than for students living in Chicago or New York.

Test for Auditory Comprehension of Language, English/Spanish (TACL)

This test, developed by Elizabeth Carrow, is an individual test of auditory comprehension, designed for two purposes: one, to assign a developmental level of comprehension, and two, to diagnose specific areas of linguistic difficulties faced by monolingual as well as bilingual children. It is meant for children between the ages of 3 and 7, but can also be used for older children, as well as for individuals with delayed speech, speech development problems, or speech disorders. Altogether, the test consists of 101 plates of line drawings, to be presented to the child. The four language categories measured by the test items are:

1. Form classes and function words (for example, nouns, adjectives, demonstratives)

2. Morphological constructions (for example, noun/noun + derivational suffix "er," same for verbs)

3. Grammatical categories (for example, gender and number, tense and verb, voice and verb)

4. Syntactic structure (for example, imperative mood, predication, complementation, modification).

The author claims that the validity of the test has been demonstrated in three different ways:

1. Her studies (1968, 1971, 1972) indicate that there is a developmental increase in scores which parallels ages as would be expected in a measure of language development.

2. The test successfully distinguishes between individuals who have known language disorders and those who do not.

3. It shows the change that occurs with improvement in the language status of children with speech disorders.

The data from the validity studies are not reported in the manual, which makes it difficult for us to judge if the claims made are justified. As far as the reliability is concerned, studies reported on both English and Spanish forms show reliability coefficients ranging from .77 to .92. According to the manual, Jones (1970) found a correlation of .77 (using Kuder-Richardson) for lower class black and Anglo children. One drawback in the manual is that the data are not provided, and the statistical procedures used are not mentioned systematically; thus, the much needed detailed explanation is lacking.

The test has several interesting features, such as good illustrations, ease of administration and scoring, its availability in English and Spanish, and especially its usefulness in identifying children with language disorders. More normative data are needed before TACL can be used in bilingual education programs.

Oral Language Evaluation (OLE)

Oral Language Evaluation (OLE), developed by N. J. Silvaroli and J. O. Maynes, claims usefulness in three areas: (a) identifying children who need training in a second language; (b) assessment of individual oral language production; and (c) diagnosis of those children who are identified as needing second language training by their teachers on the basis of the oral language structure. It can be used in English as well as in Spanish. The test is divided into three parts:

Part I. Identification: By means of observation and teacher judgment, identify children who might need training in a second language.

Part II. Assessment: Designed to: (a) quickly assess the child's "primary" or "home" language; and (b) determine if additional testing is necessary.

Part III. Diagnosis: A measure that determines the type of oral language structure produced by children who need training in a second language.

The format calls for individual testing. The authors claim that their test is criterion-referenced and not norm-referenced. The criterion they have selected, according to them, is based on the common English language structures. These structures were selected as they are common to all native speakers of English. Data were collected from 100 Spanish-surnamed, black, and Anglo children.

The age and grade level for which this test is intended is not explicitly stated, but the items seem to be aimed at children in the primary grades. The child is shown four pictures and asked to respond to the cues provided by the teacher/examiner. The pictures are of scenes from the zoo, park, school, and home, with a number of activities being performed in each of the pictures. The responses expected range from simple sentences, with some indication of time, place, cause-effect, to more complex structures that involve indication of mood, emotional reactions, and conclusions.

It is a simple test and can be used by classroom teachers without any formal training in language testing. The language usage samples collected from 100 children do not represent the range of possible sentences. In this respect, it is difficult to accept the norms presented. Also, these sentences are restricted to the 4 illustrations mentioned. More research on language usage is needed, and the test has to be used over a period of time before one can recommend this test without reservations.

In summary, we have examined a few test instruments in the preceding pages, and it appears from our analysis that not one of these tests can be accepted unequivocally. No decisions can be made regarding the placement of the child on the basis of test scores alone. There is yet another element that limits the usage of some of these tests: the existence of bias that shadows test results. In the following section, an attempt will be made to identify the types of biases that exist in test instruments that make the job of the tester/evaluator very difficult.

The Reality of Biases

The controversy over cultural and linguistic biases in language tests, as in other kinds of tests, is well-documented. In the United States, for example, the cultural and linguistic test items are based on the white, middle-class model group against which blacks, American Indians, Mexicans, and other minority groups are evaluated. Therefore, it is not surprising that minority groups have suffered all these years and were often put in classes for the mentally retarded. This has led to a series of controversies involving educators, psychologists, and linguists. Even the media have joined in, resulting in the CBS production of the program the "I.Q. Myth" with correspondent Dan Rather.

The current emphasis is to use pictures instead of language in order to reduce linguistic bias. The claim is made that pictorial representation is universal, and it minimizes those biases that are inherent in written or spoken language. According to Plaister, "Pictures have been used as a means of testing aural comprehension (auding in educators' terms) for a long time. But, for the most part, test pictures reflect the culture of the test writer. Thus, for a person from another culture, they range all the way from being somewhat puzzling to being totally incomprehensible" (Plaister, 1975:201).

This "unfairness" in tests is due to several factors. Lack of familiarity with the different cultures and languages on the part of the test designer(s); the impossible task of writing items that will have parallel linguistic and psychological connotations for students from different races and backgrounds; disagreement among testing experts on terms pertaining to testing items; differing definitions of what culture is; and, unawareness on the part of testmakers and publishers that translation equivalents in two languages may not convey the same meaning. In any case, the answers accepted as "correct" are those that reflect the value and experience of the white, middle-class culture, though almost totally inaccurate in the context of another culture.

Briere (1975) cites several examples of test bias. One of his examples involves an item from the California Test of Mental Maturity. The item states, "Bananas are ————", and the choices are "(a) brown, (b) green, and (c) yellow." Yellow is the only correct answer. For a Latino child living in a Mexican culture, the use of green is more prevalent for cooking, and thus for a Mexican child "green" is the appropriate response. Similarly, in the ghettos and reservations, where the facilities for keeping fruits and vegetables fresh are minimal, "brown" seems to be the correct answer. In essence, then, the Mexican, Indian, and black children are treated unfairly for responding according to what they see in reality.

Cultural bias is not limited only to the test items, but also occurs in testing procedures, such as the practice that requires a child to look at the examiner while answering questions. This may create tension for a child of

Mexican ancestry and for children from Asian cultures who are taught to lower their eyes as a symbol of respect to their elders. In some Asian societies, one has to coax children for a response because quick replies are often criticized at home. The mode of responding varies from culture to culture, such as, nodding of the head, uttering "yes" or "uh," and some may respond with one word instead of a phrase or sentence. Also, white children are test prone, and achievement-, motivation-, and competition-oriented. Children from Mexican and Asian backgrounds are taught to cooperate. Since the school fosters the former traits, minority children are caught in extremely frustrating atmospheres, adding to their insecurity regarding being "different." Studies have shown with reference to black children that they often do poorly in the presence of white examiners. Children display anxiety when removed from their normal surroundings (such as their classroom) and taken to an unfamiliar room for the purpose of testing. Dan Rather's "I.Q. Myth" brought several other factors to the attention of testing experts: the child may have visual problems and may not see the booklet properly, children with auditory problems may not hear the instructions, or they may just be bored and decide to doodle or draw to keep themselves occupied.

Examiners are not free from bias either. Their prejudices and attitudes toward different cultures may interfere with their objective evaluation. Bias occurs in human nature and one cannot eradicate it totally. It can be controlled, however, and this gives hope to those who have given up. Testing would be less threatening if the element of competition were eliminated, and criterion-referenced tests profess to do just that. In the following section, we will discuss this possibility.

Alternative: Criterion-Referenced Testing

Criterion-referenced testing, as opposed to norm-referenced testing, evaluates the individual on the basis of a set of criteria established by the teacher/examiner. The criteria are explicitly stated in the behavioral objectives and the individual's success depends on meeting the stated criteria. As the child's performance is not compared to that of other children in the same age/grade level (as in norm-referenced testing), this type of test is recommended by those who want to minimize the effects of bias, competition, and anxiety in testing. Before we proceed further with the discussion we would like to present Cartier's (1975) excellent discussion of the difference between norm-referenced and criterion-referenced testing.

1. The traditional norm-referenced test is designed to produce a normal distribution of student scores. The criterion-referenced test, however,

is not designed to produce even a range of scores. A distribution is not needed since students' scores are not compared with each other.

2. A norm-referenced test usually only samples the course objectives; it is hoped that the student knows more than he or she is tested on. A criterion-referenced test examines every essential behavior.

3. Norm-referenced tests are usually satisfied with indirect testing. That is, a printed multiple-choice test with a computer answer sheet might be used to test what the student knows about repairing an engine. Insofar as possible, a criterion test requires the student to demonstrate the actual repair procedures.

4. A student can pass a norm-referenced test even though he or she misses a certain predetermined number of items. Sometimes the passing score can be determined after the test has been given. On a criterion-referenced test, each student is expected to get all the items right.

5. In grading the norm-referenced test, one does not attempt to identify which items a student missed; one only counts them. So one never knows what misconceptions the student may take with him or her. The concept of criterion testing requires that each student be given some remedial training on any items missed, even if the passing level is reached.

6. For obvious reasons, test security is a constant problem with the sampling-type, competitive, norm-referenced test. But since criterion tests actually test for on-the-job competence, the student can be given full information about the nature of the test at the very beginning of the course. Indeed, the ideal criterion test constitutes a statement of the course objectives.

7. Criterion tests are much more difficult to devise and administer, but the additional time and effort are easily justified by the reliability and validity of the information they provide about student ability.

8. The last point of contrast is perhaps the most important one. If an item on a norm-referenced test is missed by a great number of students, then the item is revised. If an item on a criterion test is missed by a great number of students, the course is revised.

It is apparent from this discussion that the demands of criterion-referenced tests are greater, certainly they are more time-consuming, higher standards of performance are expected, and construction of test items is very difficult.

A criterion-referenced test would therefore involve the following: Complete revision of test forms such as multiple-choice questions since computer sheets cannot estimate a student's "actual demonstration of knowledge," or "on-the-job behavior." Because remedial instruction is an integral part of criterion-referenced testing, the progress made by each individual would have to be maintained and recorded, and alternative methods of instruction would have to be devised to suit the needs of each individual child. One especially difficult problem involves language training. Criterion-referenced tests insist on actual individual behavior, language projection in our case. This means recording each individual's answer to each question, thus accumulating hours and hours of tape, which had traditionally been graded on computer sheets!

Finally, criterion-referenced testing involves economic constraints. Teachers/examiners would have to be trained in setting down behavioral objectives and evaluating students on this basis. Their whole orientation toward testing would have to be changed. This last point will probably be difficult to accomplish.

It is no doubt true that criterion-referenced tests are time-consuming and difficult to devise, but their advantages outweigh their disadvantages in what they can do for individuals from minority groups. Pressure and anxiety generated by current language testing practices would certainly be reduced.

Legal Implications of Testing

Compliance with the legal mandate of bilingual education as interpreted by the members of Congress requires measuring the impact of bilingual education. The selection and placement of children who are eligible for bilingual education require evidence of language proficiency measures and sound criteria based on such measures. The very nature of the Bilingual Education Act and its proper interpretation are involved in testing matters. How is it determined who is and who is not of "limited English-speaking ability"? Furthermore, how is it determined if a particular program is fulfilling its mission, unless there is some testing of language proficiency and subject matter achievement in the children's dominant language and/or in the second language? (For a detailed discussion see Trueba, in press.)

In this context, Epstein (1977:60-61) recommends an in-depth evaluation of the three approaches to bilingual education. The three approaches are: transitional bilingual programs; immersion programs; and programs "tailoring a curriculum to the special lifestyles of the students, reflecting their language, culture, class, and race, 'the Cardenas approach,' " according to Epstein (1977:62).

For control research on transitional and/or immersion programs, Cohen and Laosa (1976: 161-62) recommend the following research efforts in the area of second language instruction:

1. The precise nature of the treatment. For example: Is L_1 reading introduced before, after, or at the same time as L_2 reading? What are the specific curriculum methods and techniques employed?

2. Teacher behaviors (including language use in the classroom and otherwise within earshot of students), attitudes, and previous experience and background. For example: Are comparison group teachers more experienced in teaching English reading than the bilingual program teachers? What are the teachers' attitudes toward language? Are the teachers communicating in a subtle and perhaps unconscious manner certain attitudes with respect to the languages and/or cultures involved? Are the bilingual program teachers inadvertently "marking" Spanish as a less desirable language by using it less in class than English and/or for less important purposes?

3. Students' background. For example: How comparable are the students in the groups in question? What is the relative frequency of exposure to the language involved outside the classroom context?

4. Parental involvement and attitudes. For example: What might be the effects of differential parental involvement in the child's education and in the particular program on student performance? Might ambivalent attitudes toward their children's mastery of L_1 (e.g., Spanish) in comparison to L_2 (e.g., English) adversely affect children's performance in Spanish?

5. Grouping of students with respect to language dominance. For example: Is it possible that *initial* heterogeneous grouping of Mexican American and Anglo children may inhibit and even discourage certain Mexican American children?

6. Sampling. For example: Do the sample characteristics and/or sample sizes and attrition warrant certain conclusions or generalizations from the findings?

7. The importance of longitudinal designs. For example: Is the study of a sufficiently long term to detect adequately program effects? Are the results obtained generalizable to other age groups? Are the results artifacts of the timing of the measures obtained?

The preceding discussion of methodological and technical constraints on questions closely associated with language assessment should convince us of the tremendous importance that language testing has in bilingual education. Are we making substantial progress toward the construction of appropriate instruments? Are we responding to the demands on the part of the bilingual community? What are the most urgently needed steps to take in order to meet the needs of the bilingual community?

Conclusion

In the preceding sections, we have discussed some commonly used language assessment instruments in bilingual education programs. Besides the fact that these instruments are fairly new and thus the results should not be accepted as totally conclusive, we have also pointed out the reality of test biases that influence test scores. As an alternative, we suggested criterion-referenced testing, which would eliminate some of the weaknesses in norm-referenced testing. Criterion-referenced tests require a great deal of time and planning, but the results outweigh the labor. This is certainly an area that needs careful attention. And finally, we have discussed some legal implications of current student testing practices, examining some of the research trends that are needed to evaluate the effectiveness of and efforts made in bilingual education programs.

References

T. Andersson and M. Boyer. *Bilingual Schooling in the United States.* Washington, D.C.: U.S. Government Printing Office, 1970.

Eugene Briere. "Cross-cultural Biases in Language Testing." In: J. W. Oller, and J. C. Richards, editors. *Focus on the Learner: Pragmatic Perspectives for the Language Teacher.* Rowley, Massachusetts: Newbury House Publishers, 1975.

R. Brown. *A First Language: The Early Stages.* Cambridge, Massachusetts: Harvard University Press, 1973.

M. K. Burt, H. C. Dulay, and E. Hernandez-Chavez. *Bilingual Syntax Measure.* New York: Harcourt, Brace, Jovanovich, 1975.

E. Carrow. *Test for Auditory Comprehension of Language, English/Spanish.* Austin, Texas: Learning Concepts, Inc., 1977.

F. A. Cartier. "Criterion-referenced Testing of Language Skills." In: L. Palmer, and B. Spolsky, editors. *Papers on Language Testing 1967-1974* (TESOL). Washington, D.C.: Georgetown University Press, 1975. pp. 19-24.

A. Cohen and L. M. Laosa. "Second Language Instruction: Some Research Considerations." *Curriculum Studies* 8:2; 1976.

E. C. Condon. "The Cultural Context of Language Testing." In: L. Palmer, and B. Spolsky, editors. *Papers on Language Testing 1967-1974* (TESOL). Washington, D.C.: Georgetown University Press, 1975. pp. 205-17.

D. E. Critchlow. *Dos Amigos Verbal Language Scales.* San Rafael, California: Academic Therapy Publications, 1974.

E. Catherine Day. "Review of Tests." Urbana: University of Illinois, 1977. (Mimeographed.)

N. Epstein. *Language, Ethnicity, and the Schools: Policy Alternatives for Bilingual-Bicultural Education.* Washington, D.C.: Institute for Educational Leadership, The George Washington University, 1977.

J. A. Fishman. *Language Loyalty in the United States.* The Hague: Mouton, 1966.

C. K. Frederickson. *Short Test of Linguistic Skills.* Chicago: Department of Research and Evaluation, 1975.

A. B. Gaarder. "The First Seventy-six Bilingual Education Projects." *Monograph Series on Language and Linguistics,* 23. J. E. Alatis, editor. Washington, D.C.: Georgetown University Press, 1970.

D. Ilyin. *Ilyin Oral Interview.* Rowley, Massachusetts: Newbury House Publishers, 1976.

Vera P. John and Vivian M. Horner. "Early Childhood Education." New York: *MLA,* 1971.

M. H. Jones. *The Unintentional Mental Load in Tests for Young Children.* ESE Report no. 57. Los Angeles: Center for the Study of Evaluation, U.C.L.A. Graduate School of Education, May 1970.

H. Kloss. *Laws and Legal Documents Relating to Problems of Bilingual Education in the U.S.* Washington, D.C.: ERIC Clearinghouse for Linguistics, ED 044 703, 1971.

Jane Mercer. "Sociocultural Factors in the Educational Evaluation of Black and Chicano Children." Report presented at the 10th Annual Conference on Civil and Human Rights of Educators and Students. Washington, D.C.: National Education Association, 1972.

J. W. Oller. "Review of Bilingual Syntax Measure." *Modern Language Journal* 60(7): 399-400; November 1976.

J. W. Oller and J. C. Richards, editors. *Focus on the Learner: Pragmatic Perspectives for the Language Teacher.* Rowley, Massachusetts: Newbury House Publishers, 1973.

L. Palmer and B. Spolsky, editors. *Papers on Language Testing 1967-1974* (TESOL). Washington, D.C.: Georgetown University Press, 1975.

T. H. Plaister. "Testing Aural Comprehension: A Culture-Fair Approach." In: L. Palmer, and B. Spolsky, editors. *Papers on Language Testing 1967-1974* (TESOL). Washington, D.C.: Georgetown University Press, 1975. pp. 200-203.

J. E. Redden, editor. *Occasional Papers on Linguistics: Proceedings of the First International Conference on Frontiers in Language Proficiency and Dominance Testing.* Carbondale: Southern Illinois University, April 21-23, 1977.

N. J. Silvaroli and J. O. Maynes. "Rocky." *Oral Language Evaluation.* Clinton, Maryland: Lewis Associates, Inc., 1975.

Herbert Teitelbaum and Richard C. Hiller. "Bilingual Education: The Legal Mandate." *Harvard Education Review* 47(2): May 1977.

R. B. Teschner. "Review of Dos Amigos." *Modern Language Journal,* April 1977, pp. 201-203.

Henry T. Trueba. "Issues and Problems in Bilingual/Bicultural Education Today." *Journal of the National Association for Bilingual Education* (NABE) 1(2): 11-20; December 1976.

Henry T. Trueba. "Bilingual Education Models, Types, and Designs." In: H. T. Trueba, and Carol B. Mizrahi, editors. *Bilingual Multicultural Education and the Classroom Teacher: From Theory to Practice,* in press.

4.
Staff Development: The Selection and Training of Instructional Personnel for Bilingual Education Programs

Rosa Castro Feinberg, Gilbert J. Cuevas, and Carmen Perez

Public school bilingual education is a relatively recent phonomenon on the American educational scene. The first such program since World War I was established in Miami in 1963, in response to an influx of Cuban refugee children. This was followed by programs in the Southwest for the Chicano communities and the Northwest for the Puerto Rican communities. The Bilingual Education Act, passed by Congress in 1968, was designed to provide federal funding for bilingual education demonstration projects throughout the nation and has motivated many state legislatures to pass laws mandating or permitting instruction in languages other than English for children of limited English-speaking ability. The demands of ethnic minorities for respectful attention from the schools, coupled with legislative provisions at both the state and federal levels for financial support of bilingual programs and with judicial rulings requiring various forms of bilingual education, indicate that these programs will continue to flourish.

In recent years, the number of bilingual/multicultural education programs has increased greatly. In 1969, there were approximately 76 programs funded through Title VII of the Elementary and Secondary Education Act (ESEA). By 1976, the number had grown to 425 (Molina, 1976-77). More recently, as a result of the *Lau* v. *Nichols* (1974) Supreme Court case, the U.S. Office of Civil Rights (OCR) has stepped up its reviews of school districts having linguistic minority students. Actions by OCR have resulted in an increase of *Lau*-mandated bilingual education programs throughout the nation. This increase in programs has created, in many areas, an increased need for the training of teachers in bilingual education and the resulting lack of qualified personnel to be responsible for the implementation of such training programs.

In the past ten years, bilingual/multicultural education in the United States has brought a series of significant reform movements to American public education. These movements include attempts to establish the recognition of minority languages as means of instruction, the incorporation of and emphasis on cultural pluralism in the school curriculum, the search for more valid procedures for the academic and psychological assessment of students in the linguistic minority, and the design of innovative programs to provide equal educational opportunities to children whose native language is other than English. Bilingual/multicultural education has also had a strong impact on teacher training. New knowledge, skills, and training experiences are required in order for teachers to effectively carry out these various programs. It is expected that current programmatic trends in bilingual education will continue, and with these trends, the need for trained personnel to implement such programs. At the national level, this need has been clearly emphasized by Noel Epstein (1977), who states:

> The serious shortage of qualified teachers and adequate curricula in existing (bilingual) projects—plus the clear prospect that many more bilingual programs of some kind will be begun—suggests that more funds should be concentrated on teacher training and curricula.

It may well be, then, that school principals and other supervising staff members who are now unacquainted with the field of bilingual education will be faced with the task of selecting instructional personnel for new bilingual programs. The purpose of this chapter is to assist administrators, supervisors, and teacher educators, by providing suggestions for the selection and training of teaching personnel for bilingual education programs.

Staff Selection

Both the criteria for staff selection and the principles which guide the design of staff training programs are based on three fundamental factors:

1. The characteristics of the curricular program
2. The characteristics of the students to be served
3. The set of skills needed by instructional personnel working with the specified students and programs.

Accordingly, a description of the instructional components of bilingual education programs, student characteristics, and requisite teacher competencies will be provided in this section.

Instructional Components

The instructional components of bilingual education generally consist of four major areas:

1. *English as a Second Language (ESL)*. Students with limited English-speaking ability are provided with a structured English language acquisition program leading to proficiency in listening, speaking, reading, and writing skills. Students are also provided with an orientation to the cultural norms of the majority group. ESL teachers employ foreign language education methodology rather than language arts instructional models.

2. *Curriculum content area instruction*. Bilingual education teachers provide instruction in the basic academic subjects, such as math, language arts, science, and social studies, through the students' native language. In this way, the students avoid academic retardation in the required subject areas and capitalize on positive transfer of language skills which reinforces materials presented in ESL classes. When students become proficient in English, course work may be presented through either language. Districts recognizing the value of bilingualism ensure that Spanish language electives are available to the Hispanic child throughout his or her school career.

3. *Instruction in the students' cultural heritage*. The history and culture associated with the students' native language is an integral part of all aspects of the bilingual program. In addition, majority students should also be instructed in aspects of the Hispanic cultural heritage of their classmates. Bilingual classroom teachers as well as regular classroom teachers, therefore, must be well grounded in the cultural legacy of Latino students.

4. *Instruction in Spanish as a foreign or second language for native speakers of English*. Although primary consideration must be given to providing meaningful access to equal educational opportunities to linguistic minority children, where local resources permit, majority children can be offered the opportunity to learn a second language and culture.

Each of the program components described requires somewhat different skills. The first step in the staff selection or training design process, therefore, is to identify the program elements to be implemented and the number of staff persons to be employed. If only one person is to be hired, that one person must be competent in all program areas to be implemented. If several persons will be employed, each candidate would only be required, either initially or after training, to meet competency requirements in a specified area of specialization.

Student Characteristics

It is the Spanish language and the Hispanic culture which distinguish Latino students from other groups of students. Administrators, counselors, curriculum developers, and instructional staff members must all be cognizant of the curricular implications of Latino students' language and culture background if they are to be effective in serving them. Furthermore, comprehensible communication among home, school, and community is an indispensible element for successful learning. Since language and culture are the basic tools used for communication, it is essential that school staff members be fully able to understand and be understood in the student's home language and to function within the cultures of *both* the school and the community. Bilingual education teachers and other school staff members must be able to interpret both cultures to members of either language group.

Although all Latino students will share certain linguistic and cultural characteristics, each ethnolinguistic group within the Hispanic community has its own distinctive traits. From what we know of possible linguistic and cultural difference among members of the English language community— the United States, Britain, and Australia, for example—it is easy to understand that differences also can and do exist among the members of the Spanish-speaking community. The advisability of matching the ethnic, linguistic, and socioeconomic background of instructional staff members with those of the local community is evident.

Teacher Qualifications

A bilingual education teacher should be fully certified for the assigned grade level or subject area; should be familiar with the linguistic and cultural background of the students to be served, and should be qualified by virtue of training and experience to provide instruction in designated components of a bilingual education program. A person who is bilingual and bicultural is a logical candidate for a position in a bilingual program *if* that person has had or will receive the required specialized training in teaching subject areas in the Spanish language and in teaching second language skills.

Latino parents should be included in the process used to select candidates for positions or for training programs. Interview sessions should be conducted in both English and Spanish so that parents participating in the interview can help assess the candidate's skills in the home language and culture.

Staff Training

The following staff training suggestions are based on the assumption that local needs assessment efforts will proceed and validate training inter-

A Minimum Competencies	B Assessment Questions	C Sources of Training Assistance
2. The teacher is in command of methods and techniques for teaching the language arts	What are your objectives for the course? How would you approach the teaching of reading? What materials would you employ? What content in the form of the community's history, literature, or folklore would you incorporate into the course?	District language arts and reading supervisors, successful practitioners from other bilingual programs in the area, IHE bilingual reading staff
3. The teacher is aware of the dynamics of stigmatization which are associated with bilingualism among the lower socioeconomic levels, and has appropriate countermeasures in mind	How do you plan to ensure continued interest in and study of the native language? How will you reconcile your course with the frequent attempt of bilinguals to hide their bilingualism? How will you overcome the parents' possible resistance to nonEnglish maintenance programs? What experience have you had working with this or similar communities?	Parents, students from other bilingual programs, IHE sociolinguistics departments, community representatives
4. The curriculum content teacher has been educated in the vernacular, and demonstrates competence in the curriculum content areas	What curriculum content areas are you able to teach in the vernacular? How did you gain this ability?	District subject area supervisors, IHE bilingual methodolgy instructors in each subject area

Components:

III. Instruction in the students' cultural heritage:

A Minimum Competencies	B Assessment Questions	C Sources of Training Assistance
1. The teacher uses material from the students' history and culture, both as subjects worthy of study and as means for contributing to a positive self-image	Who are some of the famous figures from the cultures whom you would include in the curriculum? What are some of the notable achievements of the group that you would include? What contemporary items of history would you select? What methods would you use to stimulate students' self-acceptance and self-actualization? How would you deal with the negative stereotypes that have developed about the home culture group?	IHE history and psychology departments, IHE institutes for Latin American Studies, consulates and embassies, community foundations, black studies director, district guidance staff

The competency statements and training techniques presented here are of course only suggestive of the wide range of competencies desirable for a training program for bilingual education staff members. More specific and personalized help is generally available from the sources listed in Appendix A at the end of this book.

Techniques

Once teacher competencies have been assessed in terms of staff training needs, it is the task of the district to provide in-service opportunities designed to enable bilingual education program staff members to gain the specialized skills required to carry out their professional responsibilities. This training may be provided with the assistance of a local institution of higher education (IHE). In the event the IHE does not possess the capability to offer formalized programs of study and/or training in the identified competency-related areas, initial training may be implemented through in-service workshops, seminars, and short-term institutes. These activities may be conducted by local consultants from the resource centers listed in Appendix A. Among techniques that have been proved successful in providing in-service training to instructional staff members are the following:

- "Observation—information—practice approach." A team of consultants, specialists in a given area of competencies, conducts a series of observations of classrooms where bilingual/ESL instruction is taking place. Based on the strengths and weaknesses observed in the staff members, a training "package" is designed. The staff member is given instruction in the new approaches and materials and can practice with the students under the specialist's supervision. Feedback is given to the teacher until the skills are mastered. This approach has proved successful in training staff in the areas of second language methodology, individualization of instruction, and first language utilization for instruction in the curriculum content areas.

- "Make and Take Workshops." This approach is used in instances where instructional materials for a particular language group are lacking. Through an intensive materials preparation session, a specialist trains the bilingual staff in the production of curriculum guides, individualized instructional packets, and/or teacher made texts. These sessions may last from a period of two or three days to a month, depending on the district's resources and the teachers' time availability. Also this approach may be used in the preparation of local assessment instruments for the curriculum content areas where no tests are commercially available.

- Cultural interaction activities. Content for these activities may include:

Dealing with negative stereotypes that have developed about the minority's culture group

Identifying areas of cultural interference between students' culture groups

Gaining knowledge of value systems for each of the interacting cultures

Using community organizations

Becoming aware of the history and achievements of both the minority and majority culture groups

Developing methods to stimulate students' self-acceptance and self-actualization.

One of the basic premises to be followed when conducting in-service activities is to make the content and objectives of the training directly related to the staff's and students' needs and characteristics. A training program is only as successful as the applicability of the skills received through the training.

Preservice Training

As initial in-service training expands, a local institution of higher education (IHE) may wish to develop formal courses from the workshops and seminars offered. These formal courses can then be incorporated into a degree program or expanded to constitute a complete course of study leading to an undergraduate degree in bilingual education. Availability of teacher certification in bilingual/multicultural education should be a key factor in the IHE's determination of whether a series of courses constitutes a major in bilingual education or just an area of specialization. In cases where certification does not exist, it may be wise for the IHE to offer degrees in a certificated area with a specialization in bilingual education.

A preservice program leading to a degree should reflect the characteristics and needs of the local education agencies in which trainees will eventually find employment. The following learning strategies are highly recommended for inclusion in the course of study of students planning to become bilingual education teachers:

1. Micro-teaching—sessions in which student teachers select and teach a concept to pupils with supervisors either observing the activities or videotaping them. This is followed by a critique session, where the student receives feedback on techniques used. A subsequent teaching session, which incorporates suggestions made during the critique completes the series of activities in a micro-teaching cycle.

2. Observation—a plan developed in each formal bilingual education course of study where preservice students may observe as master teachers implement techniques and use materials appropriate for bilingual students.

3. Formal internship—the student teachers are assigned to a master teacher for a period of time, usually one academic term. During this time the student has the opportunity to observe and practice under close supervision, the methods presented during formal course work instruction.

Overall, if a preservice program is to succeed in preparing qualified teachers for bilingual education programs, emphasis will have to be made in the areas of field experiences, internships, micro-teaching, and materials development and adaptation. Appendix B at the end of this book presents a format for an actual training program.

Although this discussion has focused on the selection and training of instructional staff members for bilingual education programs, another training task remains unexamined, a task vital to the accomplishment of the goal of providing equal educational opportunities for Latino students. This task is the identification of sub-systems within the school system that affect the progress of Latino students in bilingual programs and in regular programs and the specification of appropriate training goals for the identified role group members. Bilingual education programs, no matter how well trained their instructional staff members may be, can be successful only to the extent that appropriate support and cooperation are provided by the rest of the system.

References

The ACTFL Review of Foreign Language Education. Volumes 1, 4, and 5. Skokie, Illinois: National Textbook Co., 1969, 1972, and 1973.

Paul Bell. "Bilingual Education: A Second Look." *TESOL Newsletter,* September-December 1971. p. 6.

Paul Bell. "Guidelines for Teacher Education Programs in Modern Foreign Languages." *Modern Language Journal,* October 1966.

Paul Bell. "Guidelines for the Preparation of Teachers of English." *English Journal,* September 1967.

Paul Bell. *Planning for Non-English Speaking Pupils: Revised Bulletin.* Miami: Dade County Board of Public Instruction, 1963.

The Britannica Review of Foreign Language Education. Volumes 2 and 3. Chicago: Encyclopaedia Britannica, 1970-71.

C. H. Blatchford. *TESOL Training Program Directory, 1972-73.* Washington, D.C.: Teachers of English to Speakers of Other Languages, 1973.

Noel Epstein. *Language Ethnicity and the Schools: Policy Alternatives for Bilingual-Bicultural Education.* Washington, D.C.: George Washington University, Institute for Educational Leadership, 1977.

Florida Task Force on Foreign Language. *Report and Guidelines for Developing Pre- and In-service Programs in Foreign Languages,* 1970.

Lau v. Nichols, 414 U.S. 563, 1974.

Albert Marckwardt. "Statements of Qualifications and Guidelines for Preparation of Teachers of English to Speakers of Other Languages." *TESOL Newsletter,* September-December 1970, pp. 4-5.

John Molina. *Approved Bilingual Education Programs: 1976-77.* Washington, D.C.: Office of Bilingual Education, HEW.

Louis P. Rodriguez. "Preparing Teachers for the Spanish-Speaking." *The National Elementary Principal,* November 1970, pp. 50-52.

Kittie Mae Taylor. *Bilingual Bicultural Education in Florida: Considerations for Planning.* Bureau of Curriculum and Personnel Development, Division of Elementary and Secondary Education, Florida Department of Education, 1974.

**Plastic Man, mixed media, 1973, Luis Acosta Garcia (Uruguay)
Courtesy of the Museum of Modern Art of Latin America
Washington, D.C.**

5.
Supervision of Instruction in Bilingual Programs
Leonard A. Valverde

New instructional programs in any area require educational leaders to give serious thought to program design (curriculum organization and staff structure) and diligent attention to program implementation (attainment of curriculum goals and maximizing staff performance) in order to increase program success. Generally, in the developmental stages of emergent programs, most concern is centered on the classroom and particularly on the teacher's roles and responsibilities as well as the curriculum to be implemented. Furthermore, after an innovative program is installed, typically the focus of attention is expanded to include other important roles such as principal, supervisor, curriculum specialist, and counselor. Yet eleven years after the passage of the Bilingual Education Act, for various reasons specialists in bilingual education have not turned their creative thought to defining the role instructional supervision or administration should take in implementing and maintaining bilingual programs designed to serve Latino students.

This chapter attempts to expand the concept of bilingual education beyond the present major focus of instruction (teaching/curriculum) to encompass another essential educational dimension, instructional supervision. Moreover, emphasis is on describing a particular type of supervision tailored to provide services inherently needed in bilingual education. Bilingual education programs require supervisory behavior that will (a) institute change in staff behavior and curriculum development, (b) provide instructional leadership in identification and attainment of program goals, and (c) lend support and guidance to instructional, administrative, and community members.

Program Status and Implication for Supervision

An examination of most bilingual programs serving Latino students in the United States reveals some rather self-evident and common characteristics about supervisory practices or factors having direct relationship to supervision:

1. A large percent of Latino students are receiving instruction that neither incorporates their culture nor uses their native language, that is, about 85 percent of Latinos are not in bilingual programs.

2. Most Latino students are being taught by teachers whose heritage and knowledge are based on, if not limited to, the Anglo-Saxon Protestant Ethic.

3. The number of instructional supervisors assigned to assist teachers of bilingual classrooms is far short of an adequate ratio.

4. Most instructional supervisory personnel lack formal training and practical experience in supervisory skills and bilingual education.

5. The instructional help provided to teachers and paraprofessionals in bilingual classrooms, and others who teach Latino students, lacks adequate knowledge of Latin culture.

6. The organization established for the implementation of supervision in bilingual programs lacks clarity of role responsibilities and role relationships.

7. Administrators designated as the instructional leaders (principals and program directors) lack formal knowledge of the various Latin cultures and training in bilingual instruction.

8. University and college teacher preparation programs do very little to train teachers for Latino children or in bilingual methodology, and there are fewer master's programs structured to train supervisors and administrators to be competent leaders of bilingual programs.

9. More school districts are implementing bilingual programs because (a) the 1974 Supreme Court *Lau* decision requires some form of bilingual instruction, (b) the nonEnglish and limited English-speaking student population is increasing, and (c) federal and state funds for bilingual education are increasing.

The implications of these conditions are many, but all point out that more and improved instructional supervision focused on Latino educational programs will have to be practiced if Latino students are to receive an education that stimulates and challenges their creative talent and intellect. Specifically, more supervisory personnel will have to be employed to establish a realistic supervisor to teacher ratio, thus permitting a meaningful working relationship to be established. Not only will school districts need to enlarge their supervisory corps, but they will need to differentiate the supervisory responsibilities ranging from specialist (early childhood, reading) to generalist (curriculum, instruction). The natural growth of bilingual programs requires that various programmatic components be developed by specialists in each area. Specific and concentrated attention to each of these components is needed if bilingual programs are to evolve positively.

Closely associated with the factor of specialization is the factor of cultural knowledge. Each supervisor will have to be as knowledgeable about the particular Latino group enrolled in the district as he or she is about supervision. Therefore, supervisors will have to blend their specialization with their knowledge about Latinos in order to provide relevant help to teachers, administrators, and other district personnel. Consequently, school districts have two options for building a supervisory corps able to improve instruction for Latino students: (a) They can employ Latino teachers as supervisors and support their training in supervision at a nearby university; or (b) they can support their trained non-Latino supervisors while they learn about Latinos and bilingual education through enrollment in an approved institution of higher education preparation program.

Once the district has a trained, enlarged, and differentiated supervisory staff, then it can attend to providing teachers with in-service training, identifying and prioritizing instructional goals, and developing and revising curriculum. Before discussing the specific tasks instructional leaders need to address and competencies required to accomplish these tasks, a definition of the type of supervision needed and an explanation for its selection is in order.

Supervisor: An Agent for Change

It is a well known fact that schools are organized to socialize students and others within societal norms in order to preserve the status quo. The socialization of Latinos by schools grounded in an ethnocentric philosophy has produced program activities and educator behavior that in turn have forced Latinos to divest themselves of their Hispanic identity rather than nurturing a bicultural identity. Bilingual education is an instructional program designed to counteract the ethnocentric movement. From an organizational viewpoint, the goals of bilingual, bicultural programs are (a) making educational institutions sensitive to the cultural differences among students and (b) assuring that educational institutions promote cultural diversity by developing programs that implement a new educational philosophy, cultural democracy (Ramirez, 1976). Clearly, to accomplish these two worthy and necessary goals, some school districts will have to institute new bicultural programs while other districts will have to expand their existing bicultural programs. Whether a school district is beginning or expanding its educational program for Latinos, the task requires personnel in key leadership roles with expertise in change theory and change strategies. A natural group that can greatly assist in producing functional change is the district's staff of instructional leaders,* provided they define supervision in a special way and their behavior is consistent with the definition. That is, they must adopt the perspective that instructional supervision is a change-focused process directed at (a) promoting the growth of instructional staff members, (b) improving the instructional program for bicultural learners, and (c) fostering curriculum revision and development to represent accurately the contributions of Latinos.

School district leaders must come to realize that they will be unable to escape the inevitable change of their educational programs as their Spanish-speaking student enrollment increases. Supreme Court decisions (*Lau,* 1974, the most recent) having national impact and state legislation having statewide influence on local education agencies will continue to compel school trustees to require school district leaders to plan, initiate, and expand bilingual and other special programs for Latino students. Those individuals charged with instituting instructional change must be aware of some factors that hinder functional change from occurring.

1. As a group, educators are conservative thinkers and have a propensity for clinging to practices that are familiar. Rarely is change stimulated by educators themselves.

2. Generally, educators will ignore programs that are promoted by minority community groups. However, most instituted educational changes are politically based rather than professionally based. This is due to the fact that local education agencies are governed by publicly-elected trustees.

3. Consequently, changes or innovations are supported by only a few district employees who may be in leadership roles but most often are not.

4. Powerful community members or groups usually are able to restrict the scope of change to a token effort. Educators at all levels are fearful of negative public reaction or of possible negative consequences as sig-

* Instructional leaders are defined as persons particularly responsible for instructional improvement, for example, assistant superintendent for instruction, director of curriculum development, instructional coordinator.

nificant members of the public become displeased with the type and amount of change.

5. Most educators responsible for change in instruction fail to understand that a required change in one role demands simultaneous change in other institutional roles. Therefore, to install a bilingual program for Latinos requires more than just revising textbook supplements and hiring bilingual teachers, the common course of action to date. Installation of bilingual education means training evaluators to identify important program goals in order to select an appropriate evaluation design, coordinating the principal's task in staff development and teacher evaluation, training paraprofessionals to participate in program activities.

If school districts are to upgrade the educational program for Latino students, numerous and comprehensive changes will have to be made. Instructional supervisors in the many roles from superintendent to resource teachers, devoted to the concept of supervision as a change focus process directed at staff development, instructional improvement, and curriculum development are best skilled and well positioned to design and implement instructional programs for Latino children.

Instructional Team Concept (ITC)

To have clear goals, an adequately prepared instructional leadership staff, an appropriate perspective as to the type of supervision needed, and knowledge of reasons that change is hindered are not enough to bring quality education to Latino students. This mission is too massive in scope to rely merely on the aforementioned ingredients. Beyond these essentials, planning and implementing a bilingual program, as with any other comprehensive education program, require staff members to place emphasis on certain tasks and to perform these tasks in different ways and within a new structure. This section will concern itself only with elaborating on the organizational arrangement believed most conducive for supervisors and administrators to carry out their mission of initiating and directing bilingual education programs effectively. The following section will present the competencies and priorities of tasks needed by instructional supervisors in bilingual programs.

People experienced in the generation and formulation of Latino bilingual programs at the elementary level and ethnic programs at the secondary level have discovered that much thinking, many decisions, and a lot of support from all groups are mandatory. Also, they have come to realize that the hierarchical characteristics of downward flow of information, decision authority bestowed in administrative positions, and consensus by decree are dysfunctional in bilingual programs. In complete contrast, the instructional team concept, because its organization capitalizes on many program and non-program staff members for their ideas, forces decisions to be tied to instructional reasons and promotes staff support by means of maximum involvement.

The instructional team concept (ITC) is essentially an organizational scheme that divides the various school roles into three basic functions (categories) based on two criteria, amount of student contact and primary role responsibility (see Figure 1). According to the ITC scheme, the focus in this chapter is on personnel found in Cluster II, staff members whose primary function is to provide instructional direction to support staff members in Cluster III and to direct instructional staff members in Cluster I.

Figure 1. Instructional Team Concept
DIVISION OF STAFF BY THREE MAJOR FUNCTIONS

Major Function	Primary Responsibility
I. Direct Instruction	
1. Teacher	To guide the student's learning
2. Instructional Aide	To complement/supplement teacher's classroom instruction
3. Student Tutor	To reinforce lesson already taught
4. Parent	To maintain motivational level and cultural value system
II. Indirect Instruction	
1. Instructional Supervisor	To increase professional ability of instructional staff
2. Principal	To provide necessary environment and facilitate maximum implementation of program
3. Counselor (Clinical)	To diagnose and treat student; provide teacher with aid
4. Curriculum Specialist	To design curricula, develop instructional material, and evaluate teaching units
III. Support Service	
1. Bilingual Director	To plan program and coordinate districtwide activities
2. Community Liaison	To draw the neighborhood/school closer together

Personnel

Definitions:

I.   Direct: Individual has continuous contact with pupils and primary function is to provide instruction.

II. Indirect: Individual has continuous contact with Cluster I personnel, less contact with Cluster III, limited contact with students, and primary function is to provide direction to staff focused on instruction.

III. Support: Individual has no contact with student for instructional purposes and primary function is administrative in nature.

In addition to organizing various staff roles into three major functions, the ITC structures role *relationships* on a practical basis. Arranging staff roles on a practical basis is much different from the more usual organizational chart method, useful mostly for one purpose—making clear who has authority over whom. The ITC arranges the various positions in accordance with each role's primary responsibility to the student; thus, promoting sensible working relations (see Figure 2).

The advantages of conceiving and structuring instructional staff in the ITC are threefold: (a) strengthens communication, (b) harnesses human resources more effectively, and (c) extends program governance to more staff members. First, because of the circular configuration in Figure 2, communication can no longer be perceived as flowing from top down since there is no top. Communication can only flow within and across the rings. Also, the ITC arrangement forces a minimum of two-way communication. Second, since accomplishment of many role responsibilities requires interaction, specifically cooperation with other roles, grouping members into flexible teams is fostered. Thus, teams of two's, three's, and four's can be formed with membership dictated by the particular task to be completed. Team formation has the advantage or benefit of harnessing individuals who are familiar with the situation, including persons who would be affected by the outcome and bringing different viewpoints to address the task. Third, aligned with the second advantage, is the aspect of governance or decision making. With the formation of teams, decision making by consensus is fairly well assured. The team approach requires individuals to discuss various important points, helping to shape options and select a course of action, or to approve a final product based on group probing. In addition, leadership and influence will shift from role to role according to expertness in functional domain. For example, in a triad of principal/supervisor/teacher formed to determine the adequacy of the staffing pattern in the bilingual program, the person most knowledgeable about the abilities and expertness of each staff member will be the one to

Figure 2.
Team and Working Arrangement
Based on Functional Relationship

1. Placement of staff position represents working relationship to other positions.
2. Size of position represents functional scope of responsibilities.
3. Shaded areas signify overlapping functions among three adjacent roles. All other boundaries indicate dual overlapping of functions.
4. Bilingual director position is not shown because it is an overlay to all other positions.

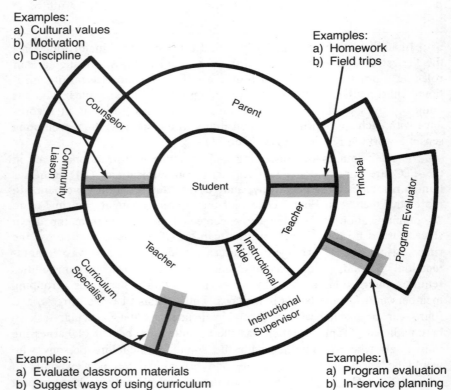

Examples:
a) Cultural values
b) Motivation
c) Discipline

Examples:
a) Homework
b) Field trips

Examples:
a) Evaluate classroom materials
b) Suggest ways of using curriculum

Examples:
a) Program evaluation
b) In-service planning

most influence the decision. Under such governance, the common situation of having the final decision rest always with the principal, who at times is not knowledgeable of his or her staff's instructional abilities and program needs, is eliminated.

The ITC provides instructional leaders of bilingual programs, whether supervisors or administrators, with a means to diversify their interaction with other staff members. For example, at times they may be leaders, at other times followers, sometimes influentials, and on other occasions minor players. Their level of interaction will depend upon their expertness in relation to the task at hand. But of more importance, ITC offers simple and clear role functions, a method of organizing for instruction, a mode of governance encouraging involvement, and demands an adequate number of staff members to accomplish the numerous and diversified tasks so common to emerging bilingual programs.

Instructional Leadership Competencies

All the foregoing is prerequisite for the prioritizing of supervisory tasks and discussion of supervisory competencies needed for Latino bilingual programs. However, before proceeding to prioritize tasks and enumerate competencies, a brief and general discussion on competencies is necessary.

Competencies in professional performance are a synthesis of many behaviors based upon general and specialized knowledge. Competencies leading to effectiveness in task accomplishment must be consistent with the context of the situation and appropriate to the target group. In this case the context is bilingual programs and the target group is twofold, the diverse Latino population and mixed instructional staff. Consequently, already developed generic instructional leadership competencies will have to be augmented with knowledge and experience about Latino learning styles and cultural patterns in order to meet satisfactorily the situational context and particular need. The blending of generic instructional competencies with various knowledge about the diversified Latino student population is fundamentally important. A simple example of a common occurrence in the life of a supervisor and bilingual teacher will underscore the significance of the above contention. A teacher who requests assistance in preparing learning activities in reading for Chicano children and receives five to six suggestions by an experienced and well respected reading supervisor may and usually does feel dissatisfied, much to the surprise of the supervisor. Why? A supervisor competent in the many aspects of reading and supervisory techniques but ignorant of learning characteristics of Mexican American students, such as the field dependent characteristic identified by Ramirez and Castaneda (1974), is inadequate.

Kelley and Teagarden (1974) state this succinctly: ". . . [a person] is competent when what he knows, does, or feels is evaluated as being positive in its results and is a part of his consistent behavior." Hence, in this hypothetical but typical situation, the bilingual classroom teacher judged his or her need and request unfulfilled because the supervisor failed to take into account the situational context (bilingual education) and the particular group (Chicanos). Therefore, competencies for supervisory personnel of bilingual programs might best be defined as statements describing the performance of skills and demonstration of knowledge specifically related to Latinos and directed at producing a specific outcome.

Before leaving this general discussion on competency, one last point, embedded and partially concealed in the above declaration, must be made explicit. In essence, professional competencies are perceived to be embodied in a person. Educators are judged to have certain competencies only after they apply their skills and knowledge to certain job related tasks. Therefore, while in the abstract competency and task are separable, in practice competency and task are viewed as one. Since the emphasis herein is on practice rather than theory, discussion about supervisory tasks and competencies will be combined.

Supervisory Task and Competencies Needed in Bilingual Programs

With this brief and basic understanding about competencies in mind, the supervisory tasks instructional leaders need to address and the array of supervisory behaviors needed to accomplish each task in Latino bilingual programs are presented. The tasks are worded so as to provide rationale and to identify the generic competencies needed by the instructional leader to promote program improvement. The list is not inclusive; consequently, it is definitely open to refinement, revision, and expansion. Prioritizing and selection of task are based on my field study assessing the status of bilingual education (Valverde, 1978). All competencies stated herein are extracted from the work of Ben M. Harris (1974) with his consent. Only minor revisions to a few competencies have been made by this writer.

Domain: A. Curriculum Improvement

A-1 SETTING INSTRUCTIONAL GOALS

Task: After 11 years of bilingual education implementation, it is becoming increasingly evident how important it is that program goals be clear and understood by the entire school district and the general community, and that support and involvement be established during the early phases of the program planning.

Competency: Given a mandate to clarify major goals of instruction, the supervisor can lead groups of parents, citizens, specialized personnel, teachers, and pupils through a series of discussions, presentations, training sessions, and other experiences to produce a report showing some of the most important instructional goals on which there is agreement.

A-2 Utilizing Specialized Personnel

Task: Providing instruction to limited English-speaking Latino students has required producing new or revising existing instructional material. Such a requirement has been met in different ways. Some districts have had their teachers make up supplementary curriculum, other districts have had curriculum writers on staff, while still others have had principals purchase material from dissemination centers. With the aid of additional funds and natural program growth, the future promises to include more specialists devoted to curriculum development. The instructional supervisor will need to provide the leadership necessary to help bring these specialists together and coordinate their various efforts.

Competency: Given the need for the production or adaptation of curricula, the supervisor can prepare a proposal to utilize the expertise of a variety of specialized and professional personnel to develop, review, and/or critique the relevance and applicability of curriculum guidelines or content for pupils with specific needs.

A-3 Guiding Educational Plans of Teachers

Task: It is essential that learning characteristics of Latino students be taken into account in preparing teacher lesson plans. Thus, lesson plans, specifying instructional techniques and content that should be used for a given Latino student group, should be the result of joint (supervisor/teacher) diagnosis. The supervisor must be involved in assisting in the formulation of such educational plans.

Competency: Given pertinent diagnostic data on pupils, the supervisor can help the classroom teacher to prepare educational plans for these pupils which specify curricular content and level, appropriate activities and materials, alternative teaching strategies, long and short range learning outcomes, and procedures for evaluation.

Domain: B. Developing Learning Resources

B-1 Producing Learning Materials

Task: Unfortunately, it is often the case that available learning materials for Latino students are insufficient in quantity and inadequate in content for meeting the total set of learning objectives of bilingual programs. It is primarily the instructional supervisor's responsibility to lead classroom teachers and other support personnel in designing, securing, producing, or adapting instructional materials.

Competency: Given the learning needs and a curricular design to meet those needs, the supervisor can arrange for the production of the necessary learning materials to complement, fulfill, and/or enhance the aims of the curriculum.

B-2 EVALUATING THE UTILIZATION OF LEARNING RESOURCES

Task: Many teachers in bilingual classrooms are not provided with information about resources at their disposal or with orientation of how to maximize the use of such learning resources. The supervisor should devise guidelines indicating appropriate use and recommend ways of constantly informing teachers of new available resources.

Competency: Given an array of learning resources currently available for use, the supervisor can design and conduct a study to determine the extent and appropriateness of their utilization, and based on the results of that study, can make specific recommendations for the improved utilization of learning resources.

B-3 EVALUATING AND SELECTING LEARNING MATERIALS

Task: Since learning materials are an integral component of teaching and learning, it is important that teachers have skill in determining their usefulness. Such evaluation skill will reduce the practice of teachers improperly, inadequately, or ineffectively using learning materials.

Competency: Given expressed needs for learning materials, the supervisor can develop a set of evaluative criteria and procedures to determine the quality, utility, and availability of learning materials, and can organize and conduct review sessions where teachers and other personnel can apply the criteria to new materials and make recommendations for acquisitions in needed areas.

Domain: C. Staffing for Instruction

C-1 ASSISTING IN THE SELECTION OF INSTRUCTIONAL PERSONNEL

Task: With the inevitable growth of bilingual programs, increase of affirmative action, and the paucity of adequately trained teachers of bilingual instruction, staff selection is a major and important task. Presently, the best way of upgrading bilingual programs is through employment of well qualified staff members. The instructional supervisor is in a good position to determine the kind of person who could best contribute to the program.

Competency: Given a description of several staff positions to be filled, . the supervisor, by engaging in a variety of selective recruitment activities, can systematically secure and validate relevant information on the applicants by conducting personal interviews, by checking with previous employers, and by using other selection procedures, and can prepare along with a committee a set of recommendations for filling the vacancies with the applicants who will best fulfill job requirements.

C-2 Assisting in the Placement of Instructional Personnel

Task: As bilingual programs expand in size and scope, staffing arrangements and staffing needs will change concomitantly. The supervisor must be cognizant of the needs of the program and should be actively prepared to recommend staffing patterns and personnel changes.

Competency: Given the task of assigning new personnel and reassigning currently employed personnel to achieve instructional improvements, the supervisor can analyze the needs, expectations, and composition of existing staff groups in various units and, based on that analysis, can prepare and justify recommendations to the bilingual director/principal for assigning and reassigning staff members to positions for optimum education opportunity.

Domain: D. Organizing for Instruction

D-1 Monitoring New Arrangements

Task: Educational innovations such as bilingual education or programs implemented specifically for Latino students frequently require partial restructuring of existing organizations for their implementation. Change-oriented supervisors must be cognizant of and skilled in the procedures necessary for such transitions in order to manage changes in units under their command.

Competency: Given the task of implementing a new organizational arrangement, the supervisor can compare actual operations with planned developments, and when asked by the administrator, make recommendations to modify operations to bring them into agreement with formulated plans.

D-2 Revising Existing Structures

Task: Presently, bilingual programs are adjunct to the regular district school educational program. Under this tangential arrangement, the functional development of bilingual programs is impeded. The supervisor should possess the techniques to identify and correct ineffective structures.

Competency: Having determined the strengths and weaknesses of an existing instructional organization, the supervisor can propose carefully reasoned or research supported changes which may include the alteration of teaching staff assignments, the use of staff time, or the allocation of resources to improve efficiency, productivity, and morale, and in so doing, improve the instructional process.

Domain: E. Utilizing Support Services

E-1 Evaluating the Utilization of Services

Task: Most bilingual programs are understaffed at all levels. By reviewing data available on staff members engaged in offering services, the supervisor can determine areas requiring more staff and special attention.

Competency: Given a plan for providing support services within a district, the supervisor can compare that plan with the current operation by utilizing objective data gathered in accordance with previously identified criteria, and, based on the evaluation, can propose recommendations that would increase the effectiveness and quality of the system.

Domain: F. Providing Staff Development

F-1 PLANNING FOR PROFESSIONAL GROWTH

Task: Continuous learning and self-development by teachers are expected and essential in continuously evolving areas such as bilingual education where research findings, new methods, and materials are increasingly impacting the field. The professional growth of teachers is a basic responsibility of supervisors and administrators.

Competency: Given a group of teachers and paraprofessionals and data concerning various facets of their on-the-job performance, the supervisor can assist them in establishing individual growth plans which include objectives for change in classroom practices, a schedule of experiences sequenced for continuous stimulation and growth, criteria specified for terminal and intermediate evaluation, and a specified period for accomplishing the objectives.

F-2 CONDUCTING IN-SERVICE SESSIONS

Task: Since most classroom teachers and other instructional personnel of Latino students receive their formal but frequently unguided training in the field, because IHE's have very few preparation programs in bilingual education, the responsibility of training staff while in service must be assumed by instructional supervisors. The most common form of in-service training utilized by the schools is the one or two day (more likely the two or three hour) workshop. Therefore, supervisors still have to be expert in all facets of in-service training.

Competency: Given a description of a staff group, including specific descriptions of their needs for training, the supervisor can design or adapt and conduct training sessions which employ specific objectives, carefully sequenced learning activities, appropriate resources and material, and which can be shown to improve the skills of the participants.

F-3 SUPERVISING WITH THE CLINICAL MODEL

Task: The supervisor's main responsibility is to provide consultation to help teachers match their teaching style to the particular Latino student group's learning style and to stimulate them to utilize these different teaching styles. Since classroom teachers often favor, and time schedules often demand, individual supervision, one-to-one conferences are necessary and desirable. In these supervisor/teacher conferences, the use of the clinical model by the supervisor for guiding the change process facilitates and structures the meeting.

Competency: Given a teacher experiencing difficulties within a classroom, the supervisor can lead the teacher through a clinical cycle using classroom observation data, non-directive feedback techniques, and various in-service and planning experiences in appropriate sequence to produce significantly improved teacher behavior.

Domain: G. Community Participation

G-1 INTERACTING WITH THE PUBLIC

Task: Latino parents and community groups have traditionally been neglected and excluded from school participation at all levels. With the recent increase of Latino involvement in school activities, and with the lack of adequate human resources (experts) in Latino programs, it seems wise and necessary to include community persons. Such human involvement, if well organized, will more than likely be a major source for instructional improvement.

Competency: The supervisor can establish, promote, and maintain community member involvement in bilingual education programs among school community members by conferring with parents and other interested individuals about classroom practices and how they can contribute to instructional improvement, and by meeting, as necessary, with community groups and leaders to acquire assistance and explain program activities.

G-2 INSTRUCTING THE COMMUNITY

Task: One way of improving the bilingual program by means of support and obtaining new ideas is to involve and train the interested community individuals and groups in the actual ongoing program activities. Such organizing and training of volunteers not only provides needed services, but the commitment to bilingual education is often simultaneously reinforced. A supervisor can arrange for and implement volunteer programs or assist teachers in this task to increase community understanding of and support for the school program.

Competency: The supervisor can plan ways in which parents and other interested individuals can become productively involved in and trained to assist at the classroom level of the bilingual education program.

References

Ben M. Harris. *Professional Supervisory Competencies.* Austin: University of Texas, Department of Educational Administration, 1974.

E. A. Kelley and S. R. Teagarden. *Some Needed Definitions.* Reston, Virginia: National Institute for Secondary School Administration, March 1974. (Mimeograph.)

Lau v. *Nichols* 414 U.S. 563, 568 (1974).

Manuel Ramirez, III. "Cultural Democracy Through Bilingual Education." *Consortium Currents* 3(1):12; 1976.

Manuel Ramirez, III, and Alfredo Castaneda. *Cultural Democracy, Bicognitive Development, and Education.* San Francisco: Academic Press, 1974. Chapter 4.

Leonard A. Valverde. "Instructional Supervision in Bilingual Education: A New Focus for the 1980's." *NABE* 2(3); 1978.

San Antonio de Oriente, oil, 1972, Jose Antonio Velasquez (Hondoras)
Courtesy of the Museum of Modern Art of Latin America Washington, D.C.

6.
Community Involvement: A Rich Resource
Marta M. Bequer and John Bequer

When we arrived in the United States in 1961 as political refugees, we brought with us a cultural background that had in its island origin almost half a millenium of tradition with well established literature and a history of more than a century of heroes who had given their lives in pursuing ideals of democracy and of freedom. We also brought with us two tiny human beings who were, too, a product of that culture and of those traditions. As these infants grew into adulthood, they were raised to live and love a country not much different from their native land and yet where they were members of a "minority" (two among the more than twelve million others of the same "minority"). Two Latinos who are also two Americans by means of citizenship, of education, and of self-determination. They both speak English and Spanish. They are bilingual and bicultural, and they do not resent it. As parents, we have instilled in our children pride in their origin and pride in this country. They do not regard themselves as fifth class citizens; on the contrary, they walk with their heads erect, not afraid of their future, considering themselves as good Americans as anyone else.

The foregoing is stated to introduce our assumptions that what our children are is what children of all Latino parents can be and that this is a very good way to make true and permanent the motto, "United we stand, divided we fall." We contend that the more respect we show for the differences of others, the more we can bring this country together.

Ideals and principles are the result of the experiences and thinking of persons from many different places who have spoken different languages. If democracy were to be measured in terms of language, in the United States we should be speaking French, not English. The foundation of our country stems from Montesquieu's classic "De l' Esprit des Lois," which he wrote in French, not in English.

Granted that a certain way of thinking is not necessarily the exclusive heritage of the speakers of a given language and granted that education is supposed to promote the ideals and principles that form the backbone of a given society, educators should be concerned basically with conveying to students these ideals and principles in the way which is more accessible to them. If a student will learn the values of democracy better in Spanish than in English, then he or she should be helped to value democracy in the language understood best.

It must be made clear that we do not advocate the abandonment of English as the language of the land. Language is a most important bond in keeping a country together. What is advocated is the notion that to speak a second language and to provide education in that language is not un-American. What is contrary to the essential principles of this country is to rate citizens according to their racial or ethnic origin, to consider inferior those who dare to speak a language other than English. What is un-American is to force children to kneel on the playground and beg forgiveness for speaking Spanish or force them to write several hundred times, "I will not speak Spanish in school," as Stan Steiner reported some time ago.[1] Such behavior is against our principles of liberty and freedom for all.

Another aspect of the advantage of recognizing the bilingual nature of Latinos relates to the Spanish language per se. For reasons that cannot be explained within the scope of this paper, the Spanish language has such a resiliency that for the vast majority of Latinos, Spanish does not fade away. Chicanos of the third generation, exposed exclusively to the English language in school still speak Spanish. This happens not only in the Southwest, but in Illinois, Michigan, and other states as well. While in Michigan, the authors found third generation Mexican Americans who would speak both English and Spanish and at home they would prefer Spanish to English. In Puerto Rico and in New York, Puerto Ricans would not relinquish the use of the mother tongue. Language maintenance is much more evident in Miami where the recent massive Cuban immigration has made it necessary to declare Dade County a bilingual county, and all kinds of transactions, in government and in private business, are conducted either in English or in Spanish.

The situation that public school districts face concerning Latino students is revealed when statistics are examined. It has been estimated that

[1] Stan Steiner. *La Raza: The Mexican American.* New York: Harper and Row, 1970.

there are between 11 and 16 million persons who are of Latino origin in the United States.[2] It is also estimated that by the year 1981, more than 43 percent of the Los Angeles 600,000-pupil school system will be Hispanic.[3] In Dade County, Florida, the current enrollment of more than 73,000 pupils of Hispanic origin constitutes more than 30 percent of all students in grades K-12.[4] It is significant that while in 1966 there were more than 130,000 Anglo students and little more than 24,000 Hispanic students in Dade County, in 1977, the number of Anglo students had dropped to 93,000,[5] and the number of Latinos had more than tripled.

If, through several generations, efforts toward obliteration of Spanish have failed, and if the number of citizens of Spanish-speaking origin continues to increase—some of the largest school districts in the country already have a predominantly Spanish origin student enrollment—it seems advisable that educators concentrate their efforts toward added responsiveness to the communities they must serve.

One form of response is for school district administrators to reach the conclusion that there is nothing wrong with a student who speaks Spanish with his or her classmates in situations where the use of English is not absolutely essential as it is in a language class. For many English-speaking administrators this may be a difficult conclusion to reach. Similarly, the children or grandchildren of immigrants who were made to feel ashamed of their mother tongue or national origin may find it very hard to accept that now it is possible to do what their ancestors were not allowed to do. Equally, the descendants of those who established the melting pot concept may find it almost impossible not to fight the revival of cultural pluralism, particularly at a time when, as Butts[6] points out, there are also descendants of white immigrants, Italians, Polish, and others who, encouraged by the success of blacks in the civil rights movement, are reacting strongly against discriminatory practices imposed on them by the dominant Anglo-Saxon white group. Those reluctant to admit cultural pluralism realize that changing times force upon us changes in attitudes. Educators cannot deal with the television generation as they dealt with the children of the telegraph

[2] *Diario Las Americas: Sera el Castellano Pronto Segundo Idioma en E. U.* Miami: The Americas Publishing Co., February 19, 1978. pp. 1A.

[3] "City Schools in Crisis." *Newsweek,* September 12, 1977, p. 64.

[4] Dade County Public Schools, Miami, Florida. *Ethnic Racial Characteristics of Pupils and Staff,* September 1977, p. 34.

[5] *Ibid.,* p. 34.

[6] R. Freeman Butts. "The Public School as Moral Authority." In: *The School's Role as Moral Authority.* Washington, D.C.: Association for Supervision and Curriculum Development, 1977.

era. Nor can educators impose on the space age youngsters the communication methods of Columbus' time. The same way television is not an evil, and space satellites are not a satanic invention, bilingualism is not anathema.

Responsiveness to input from the Latino community also implies a willingness to learn about the mores of the Latino people, their customs, their idiosyncracies. We live in a shrinking world. Less than 50 years ago Argentina was considered nothing more than a country in the antipodes. Nicaragua was a place somewhere in the world, and Cuba, a dormant island in the seas south of the United States. Currently these three countries make ' headlines and cause our strategists in Washington to spend long hours in consultation and study. People in these and other Latin countries migrate to the United States in great numbers each year. They join the millions already here. Their children enroll in our schools. In a recent ceremony at a school in Dade County, there was a parade of flags from Latin America, each national flag carried proudly by a native of that country enrolled at that school. If educators are going to provide these children with a sense of acceptance they ought to know about their lands and their cultures.

Learning Firsthand

It is not an insurmountable task to learn about Latin culture. As a matter of fact, it is no longer necessary to travel to Spain or South America to do so. If educators want to learn about the Mexican way of life, California, Texas, New Mexico, and many other places offer living examples of how Mexicans live and feel. The same is true for Puerto Ricans, for New York has more than one million people closely related to "La Isla." They also abound in Philadelphia, Miami, and many other cities. If interest is in the Cubans, there is Little Havana in the heart of Miami where the Cuban style of living is absolutely predominant, as well as in Union City, New Jersey, and in other places. Educators can learn at firsthand from local Latino residents about the characteristics of a given Latino group.

In Miami, for example, there are several programs oriented in that direction. There is the "Tri-ethnic Bilingual Program" offered at Florida International University which addresses the resistance to bilingualism in the schools and community through the development and implementation of training curricula designed to sensitize parents, school personnel, and other community organizations to the particular needs of children with limited English-speaking ability. As a public service to the community, sponsors of this program have conducted sensitizing workshops in which members of the Florida Legislature and the Dade County Commission have participated. They have spent days in close contact with Spanish families, learning about Spanish culture.[7]

Another program was initiated by an elementary school principal who was concerned with the evolution of Miami into a tri-ethnic, tri-cultural community. This program, called La Isla Caribe, features total immersion into the Cuban culture for interested students and educators.[8] A third program, Bilingual Alternatives for Secondary Education (BASE),[9] is a Title IV-C, ESEA project in Dade County. In this project, Anglo or black school administrators and counselors are assisted in improving their skills in dealing with Spanish origin students and parents.

In communities where there is a large Spanish population, principals, other administrators, and teachers should reach out and try to contact the Latino parent, who is not unreachable but may be reluctant to get directly involved in school life. Many Latino parents do not speak the English language fluently enough to feel comfortable in schools. Others simply think that they are not welcome. Such attitudes were reflected in a survey conducted by one of the authors. The study revealed that more than 22 percent of the Spanish parents responding did not visit the school because they did not feel welcome.[10] The same results are reflected in many other similar studies. Hence, it can be concluded that the problem is one of lack of affection and of empathy by the school personnel. Latinos, the same as blacks, have developed a keen instinct toward rejection. The authors can attest to this feeling because they, in spite of their many years of interaction with all types of ethnic groups, still can sense, as if it were a solid object, when someone projects discriminatory behavior. It is equally sensed, though, when a person makes an honest effort to overcome old prejudices. The appreciation of such a sympathetic attitude is much more powerful than the best conceived program and produces lasting results. How pleasurable acceptance is! How much it hurts to feel the sting of discrimination! Educators in multiethnic, bilingual communities should strive toward better understanding of the Latinos, for as the late James B. Conant once said, "School and community are inseparable."

[7] More information is available from the Director of the Program, Mr. Miguel Gonzalez-Pando at Florida International University, Miami, Florida.

[8] William F. Mackey and Von N. Beebe. *Bilingual Schools for a Bicultural Community: Miami's Adaptation to the Cuban Refugees.* Roley, Massachusetts: Newbury House, 1977. Dr. Beebe is principal of Caribbean Elementary where the "La Isla Caribe" program has been conducted.

[9] *Bilingual Alternatives for Secondary Education (BASE).* Bureau of Instructional Planning and Support, Dade County Public Schools, Miami, Florida, 1977.

[10] Marta M. Bequer. "The Relationship of Parent Participation and Selected Variables in Three Multi-Ethnic Elementary Schools in Dade County, Florida." Doctoral Dissertation, The University of Florida, Gainesville, 1977.

Parental Involvement—Making it More Meaningful

Spanish parents are frequently labeled as overprotective, which implies that they care too much for their children. Some examples of overprotectiveness follow:

Exhibit One: A new business has proliferated in Miami since the Cuban refugees settled there. A large fleet of privately owned "minibuses" transport children to and from school when they live less than the two mile limit required by law to receive free school bus transportation. Students of all grades use this system of transportation. Many live only a few blocks away from school. As a result, the number of students hanging around school is drastically reduced. Secondary schools in double session benefit from this type of overprotectiveness.

Exhibit Two: It is common to see groups of Spanish mothers or grandmothers waiting for elementary children and junior high students to leave school. This overprotectiveness is a manifestation of interest in the children and the school. In many instances, teachers take advantage of this opportunity to contact parents.

Exhibit Three: One of the authors holds night conferences with parents twice a week on a one-to-one basis. An average of five different parents might come spontaneously to discuss their children's problems. It should be noted that about nine out of ten of the parents coming for conferences are of Spanish origin.

Valuable information is exchanged at these conferences, and useful insights about the community are obtained. As a result of these individual contacts, school-community relations have improved, school discipline is better, and vandalism, if not totally controlled, has significantly diminished.

The foregoing should help dispel among Anglo administrators and teachers the notion that Spanish origin parents are apathetic toward schools. What actually happens is that this is a different kind of participation. It is not the overt Parent Teacher Association or Citizen's Advisory Committee involvement, but the participation of concerned Latino parents. Educators must learn that Latino parent participation can be increased by making the method of participation comfortable and personal, attuned to the mores and habits of these parents.

Another notion that should be dispelled is that Latino parents are not willing to get involved in civic ventures and in community affairs or that they participate at a lower level compared to other ethnic groups. A study of selected schools in Dade County found this assumption to be inaccurate. The study revealed that if community involvement was low among all ethnic groups, the Latino parents had the highest rate of participation.[11]

Several years ago, in order to comply with a court order to make Dade County a unitary school system, a plan was devised to desegregate one elementary school which was more than 90 percent Spanish, located in the middle of a heavily Puerto Rican and Cuban section. A meeting was called by the principal to inform the parents of the proposed plan. Following the American tradition, the meeting ended in a near riot not much different from what happened some years later with Anglo parents in Pontiac, Michigan, and in Boston, Massachusetts. Seemingly, any time Spanish-speaking parents have feared that bilingual education could be phased out, they have attended Miami School Board meetings in large numbers to voice their support for bilingual programs. And, significantly, the School Board, with no Latino representation, has listened.

The examples of parental participation cited here indicate that Latino parents are interested in the education of their children. The difference is that this interest is expressed in a somewhat different manner, sometimes very quietly, sometimes quite excitedly, but there is always evidence that the interest is there. Why then don't educators try to put the characteristics of Latino parental involvement to work for the benefit of all instead of trying to force Latino parents to conform to patterns of behavior they do not understand and do not care to follow?

One does not have to cite the many sociological studies conducted on societal behavior in order to prove that societies do not change their customs drastically in a short period of time. The Romans, two thousand years ago, were wise enough to realize this and did not try to change the customs and traditions of the many different groups forming their empire. Within schools, educators should learn from the Romans so that we may be able to succeed where we have failed before. If parents will come to the front door of the school to bring or pick up their children, why keep them waiting outside the school and not welcome them in? Why not have someone at the school who can communicate with them and exchange ideas or simply to socialize? Such an approach could serve as a means of creating meaningful parental involvement out of what some would consider peripheral participation.

If private minibuses provide services to hundreds of students, it would seem advisable to enroll the cooperation of minibus operators as liaison

---

[11] *Ibid.*, p. 51.

persons with the community. If one-to-one conferences after regular work hours are more useful among Latino parents than collective meetings, why not take advantage of this cooperative disposition?

Students as Resources

There is a widespread tendency to consider school-child-home relationships a dichotomy (see Figure 1) in which pressures are exerted on the

Figure 1.

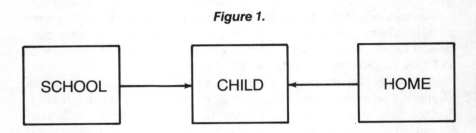

student from both sides, the school and the home. If for any reason the values of the home and the values of the school do not coincide, the students are torn between what they are taught in the classroom and what is expected from them in the family environment.

In the case of Latino children this dichotomy offers enormous difficulties. Most of the time they find that while Spanish is the language they must speak at home, mainly when the elderly are present, in school it is expected that they only speak English. In many instances while their parents have high expectations for them, their teachers considered them predestined to fail.[12] Certain types of behavior that are acceptable at home are chastised at school and vice versa. It is no wonder, then, that the rate of school dropouts among Spanish-speaking students, be they Chicano, Cuban, or Puerto Rican, is exceedingly high when compared to other ethnic groups.[13] Hence, Latinos having to choose between home or school values, usually decide in favor of home values.

[12] Marcela L. Trujillo. "New Books." *National Elementary Principal,* November 1970, pp. 88-92.
[13] *Bilingual Education: Quality Education for All Children.* Annual Report. Washington, D.C.: National Advisory Council of Bilingual Education, November 1, 1975.

In contrast to this dichotomy the authors propose a cooperative model illustrated in Figure 2.

Figure 2.

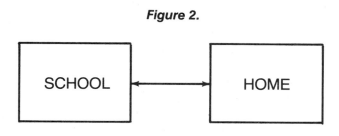

Under this configuration the child ceases to be at the center of conflicting forces. In this case the school accepts children as they are, with their own traits, their formative experiences, and their culture. The school does not work with the child as an isolated entity but as part of a sociological unit, with its vestures and its plans. Children could come from homes that are well-formed, fully functional units or broken, but the home will be each child's unit and the school will have to cooperate with the family unit no matter the level of functionality.

In the Latino setting the school will have to accept the cultural differences of the family as part of the child's way of life. The school will have to work with the whole family in order to produce a well-rounded citizen not one who is ashamed, a child who will not be torn apart by conflicting approaches and philosophies, but who will realize that the two most important entities in his or her formative years, school and family, have worked cooperatively.

The authors foresee students as resources in terms of the proposed cooperative model. When they come to school they know they will be accepted by the school. They will be able to consider themselves valuable human beings—the first step toward fruitful educational formation. But the Latino child will be exposed in school to different cultural traits, to a different language, to children of other ethnic origins. Self-assured about themselves, they will be able to accept the culture of others and to absorb, of their own volition, what other cultures can offer. They may even drop some of their formative characteristics and acquire new ones. But, this will not be a traumatic experience, it will be a positive one.

Within the cooperative model, when children return home they will be able to convey to their families their experiences, and they will be returning to a medium where there is less distrust of school. They will not be returning to a "barrio" which, in self-preservation, has isolated itself from school, as reported by Wallace.[14] Wallace observed that Mexican Americans had developed their local way of life to such an extent that they did not even consider themselves alienated from the school because it did not "belong" to them, and they did not care about what was going on in the school. They were surviving in their own environment and were satisfied with it.

Under the present circumstances, this kind of dichotomy will continue, especially in segregated school settings. A more realistic approach calls for conscientious school administrators, supervisors, and teachers working with Latin origin students at all levels to help them realize they are worthwhile human beings, a feeling that should be instilled in them from the very beginning of their education. Needless to say, it has been demonstrated that when students are proud of themselves and believe in their own potential, they are able to achieve beyond all expectations. It is precisely in this aspect of school that the student can serve as a true resource to peers, family, and community. When Latin youngsters progress in their studies, they can pass on to other students of the same ethnic group not only the example of their accomplishments but, by means of direct contact, can serve as inspirational forces to others. Most educators know the magnitude of peer influence among youngsters. Educators must learn to work with the family as a complex unit of children and parents, and must utilize this influence to dispel the idea that the Latino child cannot excel. This is the primary task of educators who want to overcome the tragedy of the high dropout rate among Latin students.

A way of assisting in this difficult but necessary task is to generate forms of school governance in which all interested persons can participate.

The Governance Question—A Realistic Approach

As indicated earlier, involvement of Latino parents in the education of their children and in their schools is not an overt act of participation, rather it is manifest in various forms. Schools are not involved in the formation of the youngster until the time of enrollment. But, when boys or girls come to school they spend a good portion of their waking hours in school activities, and the rest of their day under parental supervision. In a way,

---

[14] Campbell Wallace. "Parents' Perception of Their Powerlessness in Lower Class White, Middle Class White, and Lower Class Mexican-American Homes and the Resulting Influence on Student Achievement." Doctoral Dissertation, University of Michigan, Ann Arbor, 1972.

parents and teachers are partners in education. Some parents may be uneducated and others may have a college degree. Whatever the situation, the child is theirs and we must concede that they have a voice in the education of their progeny.

Education is a state requirement for all children from early childhood until they are well into adolescence. Other services like health care, for example, are of a voluntary nature and are provided intermittently. Public education is supported by taxes levied from the citizens, and these revenues pay salaries, purchase textbooks, obtain supplies, and construct school buildings. All of this, too, gives parents the right to participate in the education of their children.

The fact that parents pay taxes and that they have a vested interest in the education of their children brings them closer to schools than to any other institution in the community. Moreover, it is their children that parents prize most. If money for an expressway is turned down, it is to be lamented, but this is only a problem of money and concrete. When something goes wrong in our schools it affects children and parents more personally. For all these reasons we cannot deny parents the right to express their opinions on educational matters even though few qualify as professional teachers, psychologists, counselors, or school administrators. They do qualify as parents.

Because of these relationships, parents have the right to participate in the governance of their children's schools. When parents are frustrated by their inability to make contact with schools and are concerned about the failure of educators to teach their children, they are likely to experience strong, sometimes violent, reactions.

In recent years, the pressure for more community participation in the control of schools has been gaining momentum. Almost all states have recognized the right of parents to participate in the decision-making process of schools. The state of Florida, for example, has mandated citizen advisory committees to be established in all school districts. Dade County schools have local, area, and district advisory committees. Matters related to school budgets, curriculum, taxation, and other issues are discussed at meetings attended by interested citizens and school personnel. Indications are that in the not too distant future parental influence will be a determining factor in the formulation of school budgets and programs.

These advisory committees are deeply concerned with the operations of schools. Their input is increasingly important and yet Latino participation is extremely limited. A case in point: One of the authors was instrumental in the creation of the network of advisory committees in Dade County. During the early stages of these committees the participation of

Latinos was significant, and in some instances decisive. Five years later hardly a Latino voice is heard. One reason for the drop in Latino involvement was the lack of an effort by local school administrators to actively promote Latino participation. We believe that what is common to Dade County is probably common to other school districts.

If Latinos are not encouraged they will find they have been left out as partners in the governance of schools. If educators are interested in the education of *all* children, they must make extra efforts toward motivating the Latino parent to participate because most educators lack enough information about Latinos to make wise decisions affecting them.

The federal government has taken a very firm and positive stand on this matter. Participation of parents and other community members is a requirement of federally funded programs. With much awareness of preference for parental involvement, Santa Barbara County Schools in California have prepared a series of guidelines to inform parents about their children's educational program and to enlist their support. The guidelines require that parents be kept informed about school programs, that communication be established in the language of parents, that parents be involved in the education of their children, that parents be encouraged to participate actively in the classroom, and that assistance be provided to parents in fulfilling their parental role.

Educators must realize that criticism of education is at its peak and that money has become a scarce commodity at a time when costs of education are increasing rapidly. Many public services now compete for public funds. Only those showing the will and tenacity to obtain these funds will get them. The more educators involve the Latino parent, the more the likelihood educators will receive needed help from him or her. The more the Latino parent involves himself or herself, the more consideration will be given to the Latino child's needs. Educators should also remember that the Latino vote is rapidly becoming a most important bloc vote at all levels in the political scenario.

Schools are opening up to the communities. More than ever parents have the opportunity to participate in making decisions about the education of their children. Latinos, justly so, claim that they are the most neglected group in America. But resignation to this neglect will not solve the education problem of the Latino child, and neither will casual participation

[15] *Planning and Implementing Bilingual-Bicultural Programs.* Santa Barbara County Schools, Santa Barbara, California, June 1976.

[16] *ESEA Bilingual Proposal for 1978-79.* Dade County Public Schools, February 1978.

solve it. Now that the door is ajar, Latinos should step in. If they find the door closed they should force their way in. Limitations in terms of language or education should not be impediments to participation.

Anglo and black civic leaders have demonstrated that to cope success-fully with entrenched bureaucratic resistance certain skills are necessary. The Latino parent must take note of these skills, master them, and put them into practice. Those needed for effective participation in the gov-ernance of schools are listed here:

1. The need for substantial knowledge of the operation of schools and school systems. One of the reasons for the success Anglo and black parents have had in making schools react favorably to their demands is the thoroughness of the preparation of local parents. They have studied the problems exhaustively and on many occasions they are better prepared and know more about educational issues than teachers, school administra-tors, and school board members. As a result they have made their voices heard. It is very difficult to ignore a knowledgeable person.

2. The need for calmness and perseverance. Good preparation alone does not guarantee success. It is necessary, particularly for the Latino parent who frequently is accused of being volatile and temperamental, to demonstrate equanimity and to present arguments not on the basis of emotions, but on grounds of knowledge, coolness, and firmness. It is also of the utmost importance to realize that objectives cannot be reached over-night. Latino parents should expect determined resistance to their demands, but they should not feel discouraged if success is not obtained the first time demands are made for the correction of wrongdoings. The perseverant notion that "no" is only the beginning of the road to "yes" is a must in dealing with established powers.

3. The need for objectivity. This necessary skill is a sequel to the previous one. Problems should be analyzed in the light of facts. There is no room for emotion when forming a clear understanding of a problem. Objectivity is also essential when dealing with members of other ethnic groups. While Latinos encounter widespread prejudice, very often border-ing on hatred, it is not axiomatic that all Anglos are necessarily prejudiced and anti-Latino. Such generalizations hamper rather than help the Latino cause.

4. The need for controlled aggressiveness. Objectivity does not pre-clude the need for a degree of aggressiveness. Whenever issues are debated there is a time for cool analysis and a time when feelings of conviction are to be conveyed. The Latino spirit is sometimes seen as impetuous. If this is the case, we should realize that, properly utilized, impetuousness is helpful in causing undecided persons to align themselves with those forcing the issue. Yet, it should not be forgotten that while controlled aggressiveness can produce very good results, unrestrained aggressiveness can result in much harm and alienate many people.

5. The need for effective organization. Latinos have not met with much success while working with long-established school-related groups. In many instances, Latinos have been flatly rejected or used for window dressing purposes only. If Latinos are to succeed when dealing with organized groups, they should either organize themselves within these groups as a cohesive force, or organize as a separate group. But effective organization requires purposefulness. Latinos should know why they organize and for what.

6. The need for identification of realistic goals. In dealing with school-related issues, Latinos should be able to identify what objectives can be reached and what are beyond reach. For example, total acceptance in a school where prejudice is prevalent may be an ideal goal, but one very difficult to attain. A more realistic goal would be to make school personnel realize that Latinos are determined to have a role in the governance of the school and that they will persist until their participatory, decision-making role is accepted.

7. The need for self-esteem. For a long time Latinos have been led to believe that they only have a future in menial jobs. Many have fallen victim to this ego-destroying technique. Often labeled as incapable of climbing the ladder of socioeconomic progress, Latinos may have allowed this fallacy to become a self-fulfilling prophecy. Fortunately many Latinos are now overcoming these frustrating feelings. Militant groups have alerted Latinos to develop a positive self-concept. Once the idea of a person's sense of worthiness is established, that person can reach his or her life objectives with greater ease and much more chance of success.

8. The need for internal Latino unity. It has been said that whenever three Latinos get together four groups are formed. The net result of this trait is a lack of coherence, the formation of bitter rivalries, and the impossibility of any effective group work. Of all the skills Latinos have to develop, establishment of internal unity is perhaps the most important. "Divide and conquer" was a Roman adage that has been used successfully to prevent Latino unity. "United we stand, divided we fall" should be the slogan of Latinos to offset this tactic. Latinos, be they parents, teachers, school administrators, or community volunteers, should be encouraged to unite at the local, state, and national level, for as the Spanish proverb says: "La union hace la fuerza."

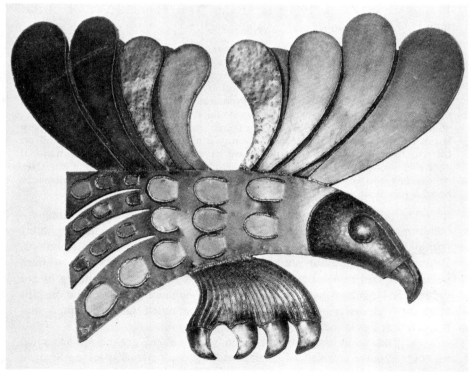

Untitled sculpture, Victor Delfin (Peru)
Courtesy of the Museum of Modern Art of Latin America
Washington, D.C.

7.
Bilingual/Bicultural Education: Beyond the Seventies
David Ballesteros

In a speech in the late 1960's in Austin, Texas, Harold Howe, II, at that time U.S. Commissioner of Education, said:

> This argument, that wider cultural exposure will help our international relations, stresses both national purposes and international amity. Perhaps the most important reason for bicultural programs, however, is not international, but domestic—our relations with each other here at home. The entire history of discrimination is based on the prejudice that because someone else is different, he is somehow worse. If we could teach all of our children—black, white, brown, yellow, and all the American shades in between—that diversity is not to be feared or suspected, but enjoyed and valued, we could be well on the way toward achieving the equality we have always proclaimed as a national characteristic. And we would be further along the way toward ridding ourselves of the baggage of distrust and hatred which has recently turned American against American in our cities.[1]

The position of Commissioner Howe was that promotion of bilingual-bicultural education would serve the dual purpose of improving our international and national stance in the area of human and cultural relations. Beyond the 1970's, our students will have more access to the western hemisphere and to other parts of the world. A better understanding of not only other languages but other cultures will enhance positive relationships abroad. And, as a result, diversity will be much more accepted and respected in this country.

At present in the American hemisphere there are about an equal number of native speakers of English as there are persons speaking Spanish

[1] Harold Howe, II. "Cowboys, Indians, and American Education." Address given at National Conference on Educational Opportunities for Mexican Americans in Austin, Texas, on April 25, 1968. Published by the Southwest Educational Development Laboratory, Austin, Texas.

as their mother tongue. Before the end of the 20th century, there will be more native speakers of Spanish than English. The factor of sheer numbers is significant in itself in demanding the inclusion of bilingual-bicultural instruction in our schools. Therefore, the primary goal of U.S. educators should be to advance bilingualism in bilingual and monolingual students alike.

Efforts to make bilingual education work and succeed must come at all levels: local, state, and national. In 1968, the enactment of the Bilingual Education Act, Title VII of the Elementary and Secondary Education Act, gave impetus to the education of the Spanish-speaking student. It provided a national means to cause important changes in the educational policy of many school districts. It gave moral and legislative recognition to the assets of a people whose mother tongue is not English. In the 1970's, we have seen many states enact legislation which provides budgetary commitment to promote bilingual-bicultural studies.

Although we have just begun to make significant strides in meeting the instructional needs of Latino students, we must not lose sight that the major goal and objective of public education should be to accept students where they are and to acknowledge individual differences. Among Latino students, these differences could be nonEnglish-speaking, limited English-speaking, monolingual English speaking, and bilingual.

Basic questions which should be raised as we plan for bilingual-bicultural education beyond the seventies are: (a) What is the purpose of bilingual-bicultural education? (b) Is bilingual-bicultural education an effective program approach? (c) Who should benefit from bilingual-bicultural education? (d) Is the financing of bilingual-bicultural education programs an appropriate function of federal, state, and local governments? (e) Is the main purpose of bilingual-bicultural education to teach our students English so they can get into the American mainstream as quickly as possible?

Enduring Concepts

Bilingual-bicultural education is a lifelong process that needs to be maintained from early childhood through adult life. Upon entering school, Latino students bring with them a culture and a language that ought to be developed fully along with the study of English and the other cultures that comprise the United States. The school must not be an obstacle but a facilitator in seeing that students take full advantage of their bilingual-bicultural background.

Bilingual-bicultural education serves five positive purposes for the student and the school: (a) It reduces retardation through the ability to learn in the native language immediately. (b) It reinforces the relations of the school and the home through a common bond. (c) It projects the individual into an atmosphere of personal identification, self-worth, and achievement. (d) It gives the student a base for success in the field of work. (e) It preserves and enriches the cultural and human resources of a people.

Bilingual education must be valued as an asset, not considered as a liability. It is not to be viewed as a remedial program. On the contrary, it should eliminate the necessity of remedial instruction by providing the student with sound educational concepts in both the native language and acquired second language.

We often err in equating "bilingualism" with a handicap or think of it as a problem in education. The fact that a child's state of socioeconomic disadvantage is usually accompanied by a lack of knowledge or limited knowledge of the English language is usually interpreted as a language handicap. Education should take into consideration, too, that great differences exist among individual children in language facility in general, quite apart from any influence of bilingualism. I still hold, as I have often stated, that the time has come for the schools to recognize that they must change programs to meet the students instead of trying to compensate the students for failure to meet the school.

I submit that the best results of bilingual instruction are found in schools having approximately equal numbers of English and nonEnglish or limited English-speakers. English-speaking pupils can learn to understand and speak the other language while nonEnglish or limited English-speakers learn to understand and speak English. However, bilingual-bicultural schooling can take place and succeed with any type of mix, provided, of course, that school districts hire qualified teachers.

A humanistic approach to schooling is equality of opportunity for all students. This means respect and concern for students regardless of the language and culture they bring to school. This is the understanding of personal learning styles of students. It is the positive climate established for students to develop their full potential by taking advantage of their cultural and linguistic assets. It is the belief in the dignity of all students regardless of race, color, or creed.

The Hispanic world has a legacy of humanism: A concern for people, the dignity of people, faith in people, belief in equality. This is seen in people like Bartolome de las Casas, the great Dominican priest who defended the Indian during the Conquest; Simon Bolivar, the Venezuelan who gained freedom for his people; Benito Juarez, the Mexican who believed in respect for all *"El respeto al derecho ajeno es la paz"*; Jose Marti, the Cuban who fought for racial equality; Eugenio Maria de Hostos, the Puerto Rican and Gabriela Mistral, the Chilean, who through their efforts in education developed a new dignity in their people. With more bilingual-bicultural instructors, administrators, and students in our institutions, I believe education will follow a more humanistic path which will benefit all our students—both monolingual and bilingual alike.

George I. Sanchez, a noted professor of education at the University of Texas and a major exponent of bilingual-bicultural education among Mexican Americans since the 1930's until his death in 1972, promoted and analyzed the dual experiences of language and culture among the Spanish-speaking people of the Southwest. He was the first to attack the use of I.Q. tests as a means of measuring Mexican American students. Using his experiences in his native state, New Mexico, and his travels in other southwestern states, early in his career he began criticizing the educational system for imposing a monolingual, monocultural curriculum on Spanish-speaking students. In one of his numerous papers on bilingual-bicultural education, "Bilingualism in the Southwest—A Tragic Comedy."[2] he reprimanded the schools for not seizing upon Spanish as a natural resource and as a means by which to bring about proficiency in the English language. Professor Sanchez viewed bilingual-bicultural education not only as a way to preserve our culture, but also as a means for intellectual development and cultural understanding.

The true and simple fact is that Latino students can learn. Their language and culture should not be obstacles to their success in school, but effective tools for learning. To destroy their language and culture is to destroy their identity, self-image, and self-esteem. To enable them to survive in this so-called but not truly monolingual-monocultural society, they must be able to put into our multicultural society other ingredients that mark them as persons with a valuable asset to be used for the enrichment of the total society. Those other ingredients of diversity are language, culture, and ethnicity. Pride, dignity, concern, and feelings exist, especially among young Latinos who are struggling for self-identity and a positive image.

"Who am I?" asks a Mexican American high school student. "I am a product of you and my ancestors. We came to California long before the

---

[2] For more on Dr. Sanchez regarding his ideas on bilingual-bicultural education refer to: Americo Paredes, editor. *Humanidad: Essays in Honor of George I. Sanchez.* Monograph No. 6. Los Angeles: Chicano Studies Center Publications, University of California, 1977.

Pilgrims landed on Plymouth Rock. We settled California and the southwestern part of the United States including the states of Arizona, New Mexico, Colorado, and Texas. We built the missions. We cultivated the ranches. We were at the Alamo in Texas, both inside and outside. You know we owned California— that is, until gold was found there. Who am I? I am a human being. I have the same hopes that you do, the same fears, the same drives, same desires, same concerns, same abilities; and I want the same chance that you have to be an individual. Who am I? In reality I am who you want me to be."[3]

This quote reflects the tremendous pride of Latino students in their heritage and their desire to be accepted and respected in our society.

We must institute a philosophy that argues that a person need not lose his or her identity in order to succeed in school, one that urges recognition of the worth of the student's heritage and culture, one that encourages development of early childhood programs for Latino children. The *School and University Review,* published by the University of Colorado, Boulder, states:

The concept of bilingual-bicultural education is supported by the insight that schools may profitably use the culture and the language of the home to maximize learning for the culturally different children, and at the same time enrich the learning for the children of the dominant culture. Thus, it is an educational tool and an instructional strategy to help the minority child achieve and grow. It is also an approach to provide a fuller educational experience in the Anglo child.[4]

Henry Trueba, responding to opponents of bilingual education says, ". . . the purpose of bilingual and bicultural education is obviously not intended to maintain the child monolingual and monocultural in his native language and cultures, not to make him monolingual in the second language; on the contrary, the purpose is to develop a coordinate bilingual and functionally bicultural person, that is, one who is capable of thinking and feeling, in either of two cultural and linguistic systems independently, and interacting effectively and appropriately with the two linguistic and cultural groups."[5]

Trueba further states: "Today there is a new awareness of a multicultural and pluralistic America, where basic loyalties to this country are not measured by the accent of the immigrants or other behavioral peculiarities, but by their effective commitment to work and to serve this country

---

[3] Henry S. Johnson and William J. Hernandez-M. *Educating the Mexican American.* Valley Forge, Pennsylvania: Judson Press, 1971. pp. 17, 19.

[4] "One-World Concept Stretched to Bicultural Schools." *School and University Review* 7(4):3; Fall 1977. University of Colorado, Boulder.

[5] Henry Trueba. "Issues and Problems in Bilingual-Bicultural Education Today." *NABE* 1(2):11-19; December 1976.

unconditionally and consistently."[6] And he adds, "In spite of all its uncertainties, issues, problems, and controversies, bilingual-bicultural education is today the single most important development in American education, because it represents a departure from the American ethnocentrism in previous decades, and increases respect for the rights of ethnic children, and a sensitive response to their needs."[7]

In the past few years there has been a continuing debate over the conflicting themes of maintenance and transitional bilingual education. The latter argues that the main purpose of bilingual education is to teach students English so that they may become assimilated into the mainstream as quickly as possible. The maintenance approach respects both the language and the culture the child brings to school and adds to this base the language of the societal mainstream. Not only is there a sense of identity and a positive self-image in not having to renounce one's background, but the values of having a bilingual and bicultural citizenry as we approach the 21st century is in the best interest of the United States.

Effective Goals and Strategies

Through walkouts, protests, boycotts, and sit-ins, minority students in the past two decades have been demanding a relevant education. What do these students want? They want an education. They want freedom. They want equality in opportunities. They want books and curriculum revised to include their ethnic contributions. They want instructors, counselors, administrators from the same ethnic background or persons who at least have empathy toward their needs. They want a quality education, which after all, is the stated goal of our educational institutions.

Institutions of higher education will have to play a more effective role in the training of personnel—teachers, counselors, administrators—who will work in bilingual-bicultural programs. It is essential that Schools and Colleges of Education appoint faculty who are bilingual and who have experience in working with bilingual-bicultural students from all grade levels.

Bilingual-bicultural education means not only the integration of students and staff, but also the integration of the curriculum. Contributions of the various ethnic groups in this country should be integrated in all aspects of school experiences: history, geography, art, music, literature.

It is most important that professional as well as paraprofessional personnel in our schools understand and recognize the unique cultural and linguistic differences attributable to Latino students. Competent, proficient

[6] *Ibid.*
[7] *Ibid.*

teachers are needed to teach students from Spanish-speaking backgrounds. Moreover, certification does not necessarily mean such teachers are properly qualified. In addition to teachers having knowledge of the content areas, they should also have knowledge of the Spanish language, techniques and methodologies, educational curriculum, and educational psychology. Teacher preparation institutions should include special sections on ethnic interest to allow preservice and in-service teachers to delve into cultural differences affecting classroom practices and teacher-student interaction.

The goals to better prepare the teacher to do an effective job with bilingual-bicultural students are:

• The teacher will come to understand his/her own attitudes, anxieties, insecurities, and prejudices in a program of sensitivity development.

• The teacher will understand the nature of the students' environment and culture (including language) through a program of teacher interaction in the school and community.

• The teacher will become knowledgeable about and competent in effective teaching skills and techniques.

In 1974 the Center for Applied Linguistics developed a series of guidelines for the training of personnel in bilingual-bicultural education programs. The guidelines describe the personal qualities and minimum professional competencies necessary for the successful teacher. They also state the qualifications that a teacher of bilingual-bicultural education should have:

1. A thorough knowledge of the philosophy and theory concerning bilingual-bicultural education and its application

2. A genuine and sincere interest in the education of children regardless of their linguistic and cultural background, and personal qualities which contribute to success as a classroom teacher

3. A thorough knowledge of and proficiency in the child's home language and the ability to teach content through it; an understanding of the nature of the language the child brings with him or her and the ability to utilize it as a positive tool in teaching

4. Cultural awareness and sensitivity and a thorough knowledge of the cultures reflected in the two languages involved

5. The proper professional and academic preparation obtained from a well-designed teacher training program in bilingual-bicultural education.[8]

---

[8] Cited in: Theodore Andersson and Mildred Boyer. *Bilingual Schooling in the United States.* Second edition. Austin, Texas: National Educational Laboratory Publishers, Inc., 1978. pp. 297-302.

According to the Center for Applied Linguistics, the academic areas considered essential in teacher training program in bilingual-bicultural education are:

Language Proficiency, Linguistics, Culture, Instructional Methods, Curriculum Utilization and Adaptation, Assessment, School-Community Relations, and Supervised Teaching.

In meeting the instructional needs of bilingual-bicultural students, both in the K-12 systems and institutions of higher learning, standards must be reassessed regarding achievement and IQ tests, admission and academic requirements, and grading practices. We must look at standards in terms of diverse ethnic groups, in terms of the changing times. We do not need to lower standards but to improve them. To require that a teacher know the language and cultural background of the students is indeed a very high standard which will create a better teaching-learning environment. The content of the curriculum and the teaching strategies used should be tailored to the unique learning and incentive-motivational styles of Latino students.

In a paper delivered in December 1976, in Chicago, Francisco Rios of the University of Colorado at Denver discussed issues of bilingual education and the desirability of considering bilingual education as a routine program for all students:

Opponents expect bilingual programs to do in two or five years what generations of traditional teaching methods did not do in the past and they are intent on evaluating bilingual-bicultural teaching methodologies and materials by monolingual and monocultural measurements. On the other hand, defenders of bilingual education point to a better self-concept and increased attendance among their pupils, to a happier atmosphere and less vandalism in their schools. But this will not satisfy opponents who demand loudly and publicly—often in political gain—that bilingual education show results now. In times of economic stress such as these, cities decry the cost of bilingual education and demand quick and tangible proof of its benefits. They fail to consider factors that influence learning among many minority children, such as high mobility in low-income areas and poor nutrition, the lack of role models, and the dearth of beneficial learning experiences during early childhood.[9]

Early childhood programs, as well as other programs in our school systems, which define educability in terms of the students' ability to perform within an alien culture are doomed to fail in the long run. The amount of

[9] Francisco Rios. "The Educational (and Practical) Implications of Bilingual Education." Paper delivered at annual conference of the American Association of Teachers of Spanish and Portuguese, Chicago, December 1976.

time spent in early childhood schooling matters little if the experience will concentrate on compensation instead of enrichment. Behavior cannot be measured on an idealized white Anglo-Saxon puritan ethos. Intervention must be done, but on the procedures and materials used in the schools rather than on the children those schools serve. Badly needed in our schools is the substitution of archaic and inadequate methods of teaching these distinct children with methods and materials that are culturally relevant. Educability, for linguistically and culturally distinct children, should be defined primarily as the ability to learn new cultural patterns within the experience base and the culture with which the student is already familiar.

If we hold to the premise that language is communication, then we must accept the language that the child brings to school, whether it is standard, a dialect, or a mixture. Where the language system is different and therefore presents a problem to the child attempting to negotiate in the standard English-speaking mainstream it is nonetheless a fully developed, highly structured system that is more than adequate for aiding in abstract thinking.

The Spanish-speaking enrollment is increasing at a much higher rate than the national average. What does this imply? The picture is clear; there must be adequate educational planning beyond the 70's in meeting the needs of Latino students.

There is enough knowledge about teacher training, about curriculum development, about instructional supervision, about testing, about selection of teaching materials, to play an effective national role in meeting the curricular needs of the bilingual-bicultural student.

Bilingual-bicultural education is an effective program approach. It provides the student the opportunity to maintain both his or her home language and culture in addition to having a knowledge of the dominant language, English. It gives security and a positive self-image; students feel comfortable and happy, which enhances the affective domain.

Recommendations

The sixth and final report of the Mexican American Education Study of the Office of Civil Rights, entitled, *Toward Quality Education in Mexican Americans,*[10] recommends actions at various governmental and educational levels which, if implemented, will provide educational opportunities and educational success for Mexican Americans as well as other Latino

[10] *Toward Quality Education for Mexican Americans.* Washington, D.C.: U.S. Office of Civil Rights, February 1974.

students. It is an instructional plan geared to the needs and assets of bilingual-bicultural students.

I would like to reiterate the following points that I feel are germane in meeting the instructional needs of bicultural students:

1. Establish a bilingual-bicultural program that enriches, not compensates. A program that builds upon the home base experience. A program that uses a positive approach which will produce *advantaged* students, not disadvantaged.

2. Encourage the students; make them feel proud of what they are. They should be able to succeed without losing their identity.

3. Provide services to the community; communicate with parents. Unless parents and school personnel become aware of each others' values and respect these values, conflicts will continue, with the student suffering the consequences.

4. Facilitate cultural awareness sessions for staff, teachers, counselors, and administrators.

5. Hire and prepare staff who understand and empathize with students.

6. Reassess standards; they do not have to be lowered, but most standards were made for middle-class Anglo-Americans.

7. Curricular materials for needs of bilingual-bicultural students should be presented positively through textbooks, films, bulletin boards, cultural events, resource persons.

8. Promote legislation prohibiting discrimination against bilingual students in the testing and placing of such children in "tracks," "special education," or remedial programs on the basis of factors that do not take into account their language and culture.

9. Make available in Spanish, as well as in English, notices, booklets, and other parental correspondence.

10. Promote cultural democracy; make it clear that all minority groups have made a contribution and that this country was built by many different groups.

The much-debated question of "maintenance vs. transitional" bilingual programs should no longer be an issue as we approach the 21st century. As science brings us closer together with other peoples of the world, it is the monolingual-monocultural student who will be disadvantaged for he/she will not be able to cope with the problems and issues of the world. The purpose of bilingual-bicultural education is not only to assure the acquisition of the English language and cultures associated with it, but to build upon the home language and culture so that our students will be able to operate in two worlds and be more productive citizens here and abroad.

The financing of bilingual-bicultural education is another issue that has received wide attention. Many school administrators still feel, regardless of percentage of bilingual-bicultural students in their districts, that it is the sole responsibility of the federal government to fund bilingual programs. I agree with Jose Cardenas, an expert in the financing of public education, that intervention by the federal government must continue but that federal funds should supplant and not supplement state and local efforts. Cardenas defends the federal government financing of programs which promote "understanding, respect, and acceptance of other cultures." [11]

Bilingual-Bicultural Education for All

Bilingual-bicultural education is a world movement. Joshua Fishman, a world renowned expert on bilingual education, studied secondary bilingual-bicultural programs over a five-year period in 103 countries and concluded that bilingual-bicultural education is a significant world movement.[12] Bilingual-bicultural education is not something new. Ancient and modern history records that people have had bilingual-bicultural experiences and that very successful programs are going on today in Latin America, Europe, Africa, and Asia.

In other parts of the world, knowing a second or third language has been recognized as an asset. Economically, it has been advantageous in cosmopolitan centers. Bilingualism has provided opportunities in the business world and has enhanced travel for many. Our Latino population here in the United States can render a very valuable service to our government in overseas assignments in the Spanish-speaking world.

The success of bilingual-bicultural education programs beyond the 1970's will depend on inclusiveness, not exclusiveness. By inclusive, I mean that bilingual education is not to be relegated only for nonEnglish or limited English-speaking students. Bilingual-bicultural education programs should accommodate the bilingual student as well as the monolingual English-speaking student. Not only is it educationally sound to include all students—both English native speakers and nonEnglish native speakers— in bilingual-bicultural programs, but, politically, we need a wider base of support from all members of our society: parents, community leaders, business leaders, legislators.

[11] *El Pitirre News.* (Aspira of America, Inc.) Special Bilingual Education Edition. 3(4):10; April 17, 1978.

[12] Susan Gilbert Schneider. *Revolution, Reaction, or Reform: The 1974 Bilingual Education Act.* New York: Las Americas Publishing Company, Inc., 1976. p. 14.

The Commission on Multicultural Education of ASCD has stated: "Implementation of multicultural education is vital at this point in our history. All our aspirations toward improvement of education for *all* children are tied to the success of multicultural education. Multicultural education is a tool for elimination of diverse forms of discrimination in regard to race, sex, class, age, physical size, and handicaps." [13]

It is vital that bilingual-bicultural programs attempt to include as many students as possible and to extend to all grade levels. While a program is critical at the primary school level, it is also very important that a liaison continue through the middle and senior school levels. Through maintenance of bilingual education programs at all school levels and the opportunity of our students in college to take ethnic studies courses, our country will be in a strong position to face social issues here and abroad.

President Kennedy, on behalf of the nation, made a commitment to land a man on the moon during the 1960's and succeeded. We, as educators, should strive to make bilingualism a reality in the 1970's and beyond: that where there is a plurality of language and cultural differences in a given community, all schools be completely immersed in bilingual-bicultural programs. Through intensive efforts and monies from federal, state, and particularly, local school districts, we can succeed. The commitment to alleviating curriculum deficiencies in educational programs preschool through university must continue and must be intensified beyond the 1970's. There can no longer be room for "deprived," "disadvantaged," and "handicapped" students in American education as a result of educational neglect.

I feel strongly that as more teachers are prepared to work in bilingual-bicultural programs, as more Latino students are admitted into our colleges and universities, and as more Spanish-speaking staff are hired in our institutions of higher learning, all will gain from this cross-cultural exchange. It will lead us to a better understanding of ourselves as a multicultural nation and a better understanding of the nations and peoples of the world.

[13] Carl A. Grant, editor. *Multicultural Education: Commitments, Issues, and Applications.* Washington, D.C.: Association for Supervision and Curriculum Development, 1977. p. 4.

Appendix A.

Sources of additional information and training assistance

1. *American Council on the Teaching of Foreign Languages.*
This organization publishes a yearbook which summarizes research findings and recent developments in the field and includes a chapter on bilingual education. 2 Park Avenue, New York, New York 10016. Phone: (212) 689-8021.

2. *Center for Applied Linguistics.*
This agency has developed criteria for bilingual education teacher preparation programs and for certification, and publishes materials, including bibliographies, useful in bilingual programs. For further information contact The Center for Applied Linguistics, 1611 N. Kent Street, Arlington, Virginia 22209. Phone: (703) 528-4312.

3. *Lau Centers.*
Nine General Assistance Centers for Bilingual Education have been established throughout the country to provide technical assistance on National Origin Desegregation at the request of local education agencies. Assistance in preparing systemwide plans is available from these agencies. Call the office of Equal Educational Opportunity (202) 245-8840 for the location of the Lau Center serving your area.

4. *National Association for Bilingual Education (NABE).*
This national organization publishes a journal on bilingual education and sponsors a yearly conference for bilingual educators. Further information may be obtained from NABE Headquarters at 500 South Dwyer Ave., Arlington Heights, Illinois 60005. Phone: (312) 255-9820.

5. *National Clearinghouse for Bilingual Education.*
A newly funded Clearinghouse collects and distributes information about bilingual education in the United States. Some of the products available through the Clearinghouse include: "A Human Resources File in Bilingual Education," "A Resource Guide in Bilingual Education," and a newsletter dealing with issues, products, research, and resources affecting bilingual education. 1500 Wilson Blvd., Suite 802, Rosslyn, Virginia 22209. Toll free number 1-800-336-4560 outside Washington, D.C. In the Washington, D.C., area the number is 522-0710.

6. *National Network of Centers.*
The Office of Bilingual Education has established a network of Dissemination/Assessment Centers, Materials Development Centers, and Training

Resource Centers to provide supportive services to bilingual educators within their designated service areas. Further information can be obtained by contacting the service centers directly.

Service Centers

Assessment and Dissemination Center
California State University, Los Angeles
5151 State University Dr.
Los Angeles, California 90032
Phone: (213) 224-3676

Dissemination and Assessment Center
Lesley College (and Fall River Public Schools)
9 Mellen St.
Cambridge, Massachusetts 02138
Phone: (617) 492-0505

Dissemination & Assessment Center for Bilingual Education
Education Service Center–Region XIII
Program Development Division
7703 N. Lamar Blvd.
Austin, Texas 78752
Phone: (512) 458-9131

Arizona Bilingual Materials Development Center
College of Education
Box 609
University of Arizona
Tucson, Arizona 85721
Phone: (602) 626-1618

Multilingual-Multicultural Materials Development Center
California State
Polytechnic University, Pomona
Office of Teacher Preparation
3801 W. Temple Ave., Bldg. 55
Pomona, California 91768
Phone: (714) 598-4991

Spanish Curricula Development Center
7100 N.W. 17th Ave.
Miami, Florida 33147
Phone: (305) 696-1484

Midwest Office for Materials Development
Board of Trustees
University of Illinois
College of Education
805 W. Pennsylvania
Urbana, Illinois 61801
Phone: (217) 333-2615

Northeast Center for Curriculum Development
I.S. 184, Complex 419
778 Forest Ave.
Bronx, New York 10456
Phone: (212) 993-2182

Bilingual Materials Development Center
6000 Camp Bowie Blvd., Suite 390
Ft. Worth, Texas 76107
Phone: (817)731-0736

The National Center for the Development of
Bilingual Curriculum–Dallas
3700 Ross Avenue
Dallas, Texas 75204
Phone: (214) 742-5991

BABEL Research Center
2168 Shattuck Avenue, 2nd Floor
Berkeley, California 94704
Phone: (415) 549-1820

Comprehensive Educational Assistance Center
California State University at Fullerton
800 No. State College Blvd.
Fullerton, Calif. 92634
Phone: (714) 870-3994

Cross-Cultural Resource Center
California State University, Sacramento
Dept. of Anthropology
6000 "J" St.
Sacramento, California 95819
Phone: (916) 454-6236

Bilingual Education Training Resource Center
Institute for Cultural Pluralism
5544½ Hardy Ave.
San Diego State University
San Diego, California 92182
Phone: (714) 286-5193

Midwest Resource Center for Bilingual Bicultural Education
Bilingual Education Service Center
500 S. Dwyer Ave.
Arlington Heights, Illinois 60005
Phone: (312) 255-9820

New England Bilingual Training Resource Center
Boston University
School of Education
765 Commonwealth Ave.
Boston, Massachusetts 02215
Phone: (617) 353-2829

Southwest Bilingual Education Training Center
The University of New Mexico
College of Education
Albuquerque, New Mexico 87131
Phone: (505) 277-3551

Regional Bilingual Training Resource Center
City of New York Board of Education
Center for Bilingual Education
131 Livingston St., Room 224
Brooklyn, New York 11202
Phone: (212) 858-5505

Merit Center
Temple University
Riter Hall Annex, Room 995
Broad St. and Columbia Ave.
Philadelphia, Pennsylvania 19122
Phone: (215) 787-6258

New England Multilingual-Multicultural
Teaching Resource Center
Rhode Island College
Horace Mann Hall
Providence, Rhode Island 02908
Phone: (401) 456-8280

South Central Bilingual Resource Center
Region XIII Education Service Center
7703 N. Lamar Blvd.
Austin, Texas 78752
Phone: (817) 566-2223

Federation of Bilingual Training Resource Centers
PWU Station, Box 23778
Denton, Texas 76204
Phone: (817) 566-2223

The Delta Bilingual/Bicultural
Education Training Resource Center
309 Milton Bennion Hall
Salt Lake City, Utah 84112
Phone: (801) 581-8643

Bilingual Education Technical Assistance Center
708 South G St.
Tacoma, Washington 98405
Phone: (206) 593-6980

Bilingual Training Resource Center
406 Hall of Health
G.S. 25
University of Washington
Seattle, Washington 98115
Phone: (206) 543-9424

7. *State Affiliates of the National Association for Bilingual Education (NABE).*

Several states have organized state affiliates of NABE. They provide a variety of services in bilingual education to local members. A list of the affiliates and local contact persons can be obtained through the NABE headquarters.

8. *State Education Departments.*

Several states have added bilingual education divisions to their departments of education. States with Title VII or Title IV programs also receive special federal funds to provide technical assistance to school districts. In other states, the foreign language or language arts consultants may be of assistance.

9. *Teachers of English to Speakers of Other Languages (TESOL).*

This national organization periodically publishes guidelines for teacher preparation programs for Teachers of English as a Second Language which may be useful in the selection process. Lists of publications and names of local members of the organization who may be able to serve as consultants are available from TESOL, Georgetown University, 455 Nevils, Washington, D.C. 20057. Phone: (202) 337-7264.

Appendix B. PLAN FOR PROVIDING TRAINING

OBJECTIVES	METHODS	SELECTION OF PERSONNEL	RATIONALE AND EXPECTED CONTENT	EVALUATION	PROPOSED TIMETABLES
1. To familiarize instructional personnel and community with the philosophy, goals, and the method of selection and instruction of the students.	1. Participation in teacher and staff meetings, principals' meetings, and parents' meetings. 2. News media will be used to disseminate information regarding the program to the public. Bilingual office will send invitations to community leaders to participate in special programs.	All personnel in schools where bilingual program will be conducted	Will include review of philosophy and goals of program. Audio-visual material on bilingual program in operation in the county, methods of selection of students, etc.	Teachers will become more knowledgeable in the method of instruction and selection of students participating in the program. There will be 8 staff meetings, 4 parent meetings, and monthly meetings with the Bilingual Program Advisory Committee. A random survey will be conducted to ascertain the effectiveness of orientation program. News media understanding of and participation in the programs will be evaluated in terms of the number of writeups and allotted time given to the program on the air.	Sept. 16 Nov. 30 Newsmedia information dissemination is ongoing.
2. To familiarize school personnel with specific information about parallel cultures and with the impact of these aspects of cultures on the student(s) progress in the school system.	1. Bilingual Program Advisory Committee will be formed.	This committee will be composed of interested parents, community leaders, representatives of the news media, counselors, and teachers.		This knowledge will facilitate the selection of appropriate educational materials and help the instructional personnel develop a better understanding of the target students' cultures, educational achievement and behavior patterns.	Yearlong, ongoing

OBJECTIVES	METHODS	SELECTION OF PERSONNEL	RATIONALE AND EXPECTED CONTENT	EVALUATION	PROPOSED TIMETABLES
	2. Booklets and other pertinent materials will be made available to each school. These will include information on education and culture differences.	These materials will be given to: 1. All personnel in the programs. 2. All principals 3. Resource Room in Media Center 4. Other key personnel	1. An explanation of the effect of cultural differences for each linguistic/ethnic group. 2. Experiences which will facilitate the understanding of and positive attitudes toward members of minority groups.	This will be accomplished through classroom observation of teacher behavior conducted by the Coordinator, Bilingual Program. A self-report questionnaire will be available to all workshop participants.	October 31 December 19

OBJECTIVES	METHODS	SELECTION OF PERSONNEL	RATIONALE AND EXPECTED CONTENT	EVALUATION	PROPOSED TIMETABLES
3. To familiarize with and increase the competency of the instructional personnel in identification, development, and use of instructional materials for each group for: 1. Bilingual Program 2. ESL 3. Native language literacy 4. Math, social studies, science, and native language instruction.	1. Different companies will present, demonstrate and explain their programs of ESL instruction and their bilingual programs. 2. Consultants will be contracted to provide instruction in the development of materials. Such materials will aid in individualizing the instruction of the target students in the various languages.	All personnel in the bilingual program will be involved. Workshops will be divided according to grade levels.	All the personnel involved with the bilingual program will be thoroughly familiar with the materials and resources available to help them implement their curriculum. These personnel will in turn be able to train newcomers to the program.	1. The program will show evidence of appropriate commercially prepared materials which have been identified by the workshop participants. 2. Replications of the materials developed by participants. 3. Outside evaluators.	Ongoing program throughout the year.

OBJECTIVES	METHODS	SELECTION OF PERSONNEL	RATIONALE AND EXPECTED CONTENT	EVALUATION	PROPOSED TIMETABLES
4. To familiarize personnel with instructional methodologies and techniques in the various subject areas to be taught in the native language and for ESL.	1. This will be accomplished through the use of audiovisual demonstrations, classroom observations, lectures, and year long workshops. 2. Curriculum guides for all grade levels and subject areas will be made available to all instructional personnel in the program.	All instructional personnel in the program who are teaching in the identified languages. The group will be divided into secondary and elementary levels.	All instructional personnel in this program will have gained a greater understanding and knowledge of methods and techniques involved in teaching target students. They will also be familiar with the content and county requirements of each subject area.	1. Observations and evaluations of the instructional personnel in the program in the implementation and application of the methodology and techniques will be conducted by subject area supervisors. 2. Participants will be able to increase their performance in a pre- and post-test developed by the consultants.	Year-long ongoing program to start in January.

OBJECTIVES	METHODS	SELECTION OF PERSONNEL	RATIONALE AND EXPECTED CONTENT	EVALUATION	PROPOSED TIMETABLES
5. To develop staff capacity to familiarize the target student and family with community resources and job opportunities.	The counselors will inform the target student and family of community resources and job opportunities through individual and group sessions, home visitations and P.T.A. meetings. A slide presentation will be prepared in the various languages of the target student(s) showing the aforementioned.	Target student, family, and instructional personnel in the bilingual program.	Through these activities the target student, family and the instructional personnel will become knowledgeable of the resources available in the community and the job opportunities available to the bilingual/bicultural person.	The number of requests for community services will increase. The number of referrals of bilingual families and community resources will increase.	Ongoing year-long project to start in January.

Appendix B.

Sections from an in-service training plan developed under the direction of Norma LoBato, Bilingual Education Coordinator, Hillsborough County Schools, with the assistance of Gilbert Cuevas and Rosa Castro Feinberg, are presented here as a guide to the organization of staff training plans.

About the Authors

DAVID BALLESTEROS, Vice Chancellor for Academic Affairs at the University of Colorado at Colorado Springs, holds B.A. and M.A. degrees in Spanish and a Ph.D. in Latin American Studies. He has served as a consultant in bilingual education at the federal, state, and local levels, and has lectured in the area of multicultural education in various colleges and universities in the United States and Mexico.

JOHN BEQUER holds a Ph.D. from the University of Michigan, a Master's in Law from the University of Havana, a Master's in Education from Eastern Michigan University, and a Bachelor's from the University of Havana. Presently, he is the principal of Kinlock Park Junior High School, Dade County Public Schools, Florida.

MARTA M. BEQUER holds a Doctorate in Education from the University of Florida and from the University of Havana, and a Master's in Education from the University of Miami. Presently, she is the Administrative Assistant to the Superintendent of the Dade County Public Schools, Florida.

GILBERT CUEVAS is the Coordinator of teacher training programs in bilingual education at the University of Miami. He is currently conducting research in the area of mathematical concept development. He is also a consultant for the Miami *Lau* Center.

RITA DEYOE is currently Managing Editor at the Center for the Development of Bilingual Curriculum, Dallas, and Adjunct Assistant Professor of Bilingual Elementary Education at East Texas State University.

ROSA CASTRO FEINBERG is the Associate Director of the University of Miami General Assistance Center for Bilingual Education. Her expertise is in *Lau* compliance, bilingual education, and administration and curriculum. She was previously employed by the Dade County Public Schools.

MELITON LOPEZ is currently Assistant Superintendent for Curriculum and Instruction for the Chula Vista Elementary School District near San Diego, California. He has been among the "pioneers" in bilingual education in California and the Southwest. He received his Doctorate from Wayne State University in 1972.

CARMEN A. PEREZ is the Project Director of the Bilingual Education Program at the State University of New York at Albany.

KAMAL K. SHIDHAR is a Visiting Assistant Professor in the Department of Educational Psychology and Bilingual/Bicultural Education at the University of Illinois. Her areas of expertise include bilingualism/multilingualism, ESL, Language Testing, and Sociolinguistics. She is currently analyzing data regarding the language usage by bilinguals/multilinguals in various social and educational settings in India.

JUAN DE DIOS SOLIS has taught at the elementary and secondary levels for eleven years. He has held administrative positions with the Texas Education Agency and currently is the Director of the National Center for the Development of Bilingual Curriculum, Dallas. Also, he is the President of the National Association for Bilingual Education.

HENRY T. TRUEBA has been in the Department of Secondary Education at the University of Illinois since 1973. He is the director of the Office of Multilingual Bilingual Education, and of the Midwest Office for Materials Development. He has published several articles and books in the area of bilingual education. Currently, he is editing four books scheduled for publication during 1978. He is the founder and president of the National Association of Colleges and Universities for Bilingual Education (NACUBE).

LEONARD A. VALVERDE is Assistant Professor of Educational Administration and Director of the Instructional Supervision Program at the University of Texas at Austin. His research and publications have centered on educational equity questions having implications for Latino students in urban schools and higher education institutions. He is the chairperson of the ASCD Latino Working Group on Bilingual Education.